Reading Response Road Maps

by Tracy Fasick

New York • Toronto • London • Auckland • Sydney
Mexico City • New Delhi • Hong Kong • Buenos Aires

Teaching
Resources

Dedication

To my family and friends who have supported me; you know who you are.

And to my teaching mentor, Ellen Hollingshead—the profession misses you!

Produced and edited by Immacula A. Rhodes
Cover design by Jason Robinson
Interior design and illustrations by Sydney Wright

ISBN: 978-0-545-26711-3

2 3 4 5 6 7 8 9 10   40   18 17 16 15 14 13 12

Contents

Reading Response Road Maps

Contents

(continued)

Contents

(continued)

Introduction

Welcome to *Reading Response Road Maps!* This collection of 50 fun, innovative "road maps" helps strengthen reading skills and boost comprehension by prompting students to stop and think about what they read. Each map is connected to a popular picture book and is designed to help students develop effective thought processes and strategies that build and reinforce key comprehension skills as they journey through the book.

According to the National Reading Panel (NRP), text comprehension is one of the five essential components of effective reading instruction, which also includes phonemic awareness, phonics, fluency, and vocabulary. From their analysis of more than 200 studies, the NRP (2000) concluded that using the following strategies enhanced the comprehension of average readers: monitoring comprehension, cooperative learning, graphic organizers, story structure, answering and generating questions, summarizing, and multiple strategy instruction. Teaching students strategies for answering or generating questions of their own—before, during, and after reading—is extremely important in helping them improve their comprehension (NRP, 2000). Questions allow students to monitor their understanding of text, engage with a piece of text, and construct memory representations as they read. Evidence also exists to support cooperative or collaborative learning with peers in order to improve comprehension (Fuchs et al, 1997; Vaughn & Klinger, 1999).

The reading road maps in this book use the instructional strategies of questioning and cooperative learning to help guide students in their overall comprehension of text. Students follow a road map while reading passages in the corresponding picture book. Along the way, they stop to respond to a variety of prompts related to what they have just read. The game-like, interactive format encourages students to use important skills that boost comprehension, such as activating prior knowledge, analyzing characters, recalling events, making predictions and inferences, identifying cause-and-effect relationships, and making personal connections.

The reproducible maps are ready to go and easy to use. They can be used with the whole class, small groups, or as partner activities. To further reinforce comprehension, you might use the maps with individual students. In addition, you can make a school-home connection by sending the maps home for students to share with their families.

As students work with peers to navigate the reading road maps, they are given the opportunity to think, talk, and even write about what they have read. Fun art and meaningful prompts make them the perfect motivational tool to help improve comprehension. You may even find that using the maps helps boost students' comprehension scores on both standardized and local reading assessments. Once students get on the road to reading success with these maps, they'll be asking for more. So get out a map and enjoy the journey!

About This Book

What Is a Reading Response Road Map?

A reading road map is simply a navigated journey through a picture book. Prompts in text boxes, along with art cues, help guide students' comprehension about what they read as they travel through the story. After students read a targeted passage, stop to read and respond to the corresponding prompt on the map. The prompts are designed to help students recall events, describe characters, predict outcomes, explore cause-and-effect relationships, and make personal connections, among other comprehension-building strategies. By talking about ideas in the text, students demonstrate their ability to read for meaning and engage in solving problems.

The books and corresponding maps in this resource are organized progressively from simple—and sometimes repetitive—text to more complex text structures and vocabulary. "One of the key requirements of the Common Core State Standards for Reading is that all students must be able to comprehend texts of steadily increasing complexity as they progress through school." (Common Core State Standards, 2011). The sequence of books in the table of contents allows you to choose from a wide range of levels to match students' reading ability. As stated by Irene Fountas and Gay Su Pinnell in *Guided Reading: Good First Teaching for All Children*, "We want to be sure children are working with materials that help them take the next step in learning to read. The books they read should offer just enough challenge to support problem solving but be easy enough to support fluency and meaning" (p. xvi, 1996). The maps also serve as useful tools for differentiating instruction and guiding students to reading success.

> ## Meeting the English Language Arts Standards
>
> The Common Core State Standards Initiative (CCSSI) has outlined learning expectations in language arts for students at different grade levels. The activities in this book align with the Reading, Speaking & Listening, and Language standards for students in Kindergarten through grade 2. For more information, see the chart on page 12.

Using the Reading Response Road Maps

The reproducible, reading response road maps in this book are ready to go. Simply copy the map of your choice, color it (if desired), and it's ready for use. Whether you are teaching the whole class or a small group, or students are working independently, the first step is to read the caption at the top left to discover the purpose of the journey. In most cases, the map will connect one character to another character or to a specific place at the end of the path. Then begin the journey at the arrow labeled "Start here." Follow the path, reading the directions in each text box along the way and stopping after reading the passage in the book to respond to the prompt. Notice that some picture books have page numbers, but most do not. For those books, the first page that contains story text is counted as page 1 on the map (even if art for the beginning of the story spans a two-page spread). So, page 1 may begin on a left-hand or a right-hand page. Continue traveling along the path until the end, writing a check in the circle at the top left corner of each text box after responding to the prompt.

One attribute of the reading road maps is that you can use them in many ways and for different purposes to build students' comprehension skills. The fun, game-like format motivates students to interact with text as they work their way through picture books. To introduce each map, follow the directions on the map to read the story and guide students through the prompts. As you travel along, model the thinking and questioning strategies included on the map,

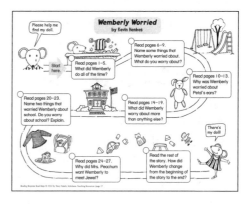

using a think-aloud approach to respond to each prompt. This method works well for whole-class and small-group guided reading activities, as well as for preparing students to use the maps for partner or independent reading. The maps can also be used effectively as an assessment tool or to establish school-home connections that encourage families to interact in a fun, meaningful way with their children.

Helpful Hints

❋ Color and laminate the reading road maps. Then use a wipe-off pen to check off the prompts as students give their responses.

❋ Copy the map onto a transparency. Use an overhead projector to display the map for whole-class or small-group instruction.

❋ To make a game version, provide counters for use as game markers. Then place the map on a table to use as a game board. Invite students to place their game markers on the Start arrow and then move them along the path as they respond to each prompt.

❋ Have paper and pencils handy for students to write their responses to the prompts, if desired.

❋ After students are familiar with a story and its map, put the book, a laminated copy of the map, and a wipe-off pen in a zippered plastic bag to create a "mini-center" for use as an independent or partner reading activity.

Suggestions for Using the Reading Response Road Maps

Following are some suggestions on ways you might use the reading road maps:

❋ Read the questions together with students and check that they know what they will be looking for prior to reading a passage.

❋ Check off each text box as students read and respond to the prompt. Encourage students to do the same when working through the maps with partners or independently.

❋ When using the map with small groups or pairs, have students take turns responding to the prompts along the path. Then invite all students to talk about the response and to share additional thoughts and ideas.

❋ Encourage students to respond orally, in writing, or by both methods to provide additional reinforcement in comprehension. To record their responses, have students pause between each prompt to write their answers and ideas on paper. Ask them to jot down the page ranges to use as a reference when reviewing the story.

* When working with small groups or individuals who might need scaffolding, model reading and answering the first question or two together. Then provide additional support, as needed, as students finish reading and completing the activity.

* Monitor student responses, modeling comprehension-building strategies as needed as students interact with the story and prompts. This will provide students with valuable guided practice to help prepare them for using the maps more independently with partners or individually. It will also help you assess students' use of comprehension skills and strategies.

* Ask students to record their responses on paper. You can use the written responses as another tool for assessing students' understanding of what they read.

* If using a road map as an independent reading activity, give each student a copy of the map to color and personalize. Have students check off the prompts as they complete them while navigating the story.

* Send the road maps and corresponding books home with students to share with their families. This is an excellent way to involve parents in helping their children develop and improve essential reading skills. It can also help keep families informed of their children's progress and any areas that need additional work.

References and Resources

Common Core State Standards for English Language Arts & Literacy in History/Social Studies, Science, and Technical Subjects, Appendix A, 2011.

Fountas, I. & Pinnell G. (1996). *Guided reading: Good first teaching for all children.* New Hampshire, Heinemann.

Fuchs, D., Fuchs, L. S., Mathes, P. G., & Simmons, D. C. (1997). "Peer-assisted learning strategies: Making classrooms more responsive to diversity." *American Educational Research Journal*, 34, 174–206.

National Institute of Child Health and Human Development (NICHD). (2000). Report of the National Reading Panel. *Teaching children to read: An evidence-based assessment of the scientific research literature on reading and its implications for reading instruction.* Washington, DC: National Institutes of Health (NIH). Retrieved June 23, 2009, from http://www.nationalereadingpanel.org/Publications/summary.htm

Reeves, D. (2010). "The write way." *American School Board Journal*, 197 (11) p. 46–47.

Vaughn, S., & Klinger, J. K. (1999). "Teaching reading comprehension through collaborative strategic reading." *Intervention in School and Clinic*, 34, 284–292.

Extension Activities

After using the reading response road maps, keep the learning going with these extension activities that can be used with any picture book in this resource. Each activity allows students to express an understanding of key elements and concepts by demonstrating their comprehension through writing. Research findings have concluded students' reading test scores improve as their writing improves (Reeves, 2010). When using the activities, you might have students complete the writing portion of each task before doing the artwork or illustrations.

Book Jacket: Have students design a book jacket. First, ask them to fold a sheet of construction paper in half. With the fold to the left, have them write the book title and author on the front cover and add an illustration. Then instruct students to open their cover. On the left side, have them write a summary about the story. On the right, ask them tell whether or not they would recommend the story to a friend and to explain why. Also, have them write a sentence or two about their favorite part of the story and illustrate it. After completing the interior, ask students to turn to the back cover and write a leading question that would draw the attention of other readers to the story. To display, stand the book jackets upright on a flat surface.

Puzzle Review: In this activity, students create puzzles to demonstrate their comprehension of story events, concepts, or ideas. First, ask them to draw a scene related to the story on a sheet of construction paper. When finished, have them flip the paper over and draw lines to create several puzzle pieces on the back, making sure each piece is large enough to write a sentence on. The number of pieces will depend on student ability levels and the information you want them to include on the pieces. For example, emergent readers might create three 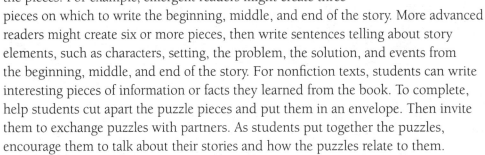 pieces on which to write the beginning, middle, and end of the story. More advanced readers might create six or more pieces, then write sentences telling about story elements, such as characters, setting, the problem, the solution, and events from the beginning, middle, and end of the story. For nonfiction texts, students can write interesting pieces of information or facts they learned from the book. To complete, help students cut apart the puzzle pieces and put them in an envelope. Then invite them to exchange puzzles with partners. As students put together the puzzles, encourage them to talk about their stories and how the puzzles relate to them.

Retelling Bag: Distribute plain paper bags for students to decorate and use in retelling a story. First, have students write a summary or their own opinion of the story on one side of the bag. Or, ask them to write about the story problem, solution, beginning, middle, and end of the story on separate index cards, which they place in the bag. For nonfiction text, students can write facts or interesting information they learned from the book on the index cards. Once they've finished writing, have students illustrate the other side of their bag with a character, scene, or significant event from the story. Finally, invite students to retell the story using their bags and text (or index cards) as prompts to demonstrate comprehension of the story.

Story Game Board: Help students use geometric shape cutouts to create a story-related game board. They can glue the shapes inside a manila file folder to create a simple path, then label a few of the shapes with directions, such as "Move ahead 1 space," "Skip a turn," and "Move back 2 spaces." Have them also label the end spaces of their path with either "Start" or "Finish." Then have students write questions about the story on individual index cards. The number of questions might vary based on the story, student ability levels, and the need for differentiation. To play the game, shuffle the cards and place them facedown. Have players flip a penny to determine the number of spaces they'll move on their turn: If heads, move 2 spaces; if tails, move one. Ask players to follow the directions on the space they land on. If they land on a blank space, they pick a card and answer the question. If correct, they stay on that space. Otherwise, they return to their previous space. The first player to reach Finish wins the game.

Character Book: Students' creativity can soar with this activity! Ask students to choose a character from a fiction or nonfiction book they've read to create a character book. To begin, have them fold the two short ends of a sheet of construction paper toward each other until they meet in the center. After creasing the folds, ask students to unfold the paper and write a story summary or character analysis on the inside sections. (If using dark construction paper, have students write their text on white paper, then glue the page onto the dark paper inside the folded area.) When finished, have students refold the paper. Explain that this will become the body of their character book—readers will be able to open this section to read about the story or character. To complete their book, invite students to create a head, limbs, tail, or other features to attach to the body to make it resemble their character. Then invite students to share the text they've written inside the body section of their book with the class. Afterward, encourage students to discuss the book and share their own ideas about it.

Make Your Own Reading Response Road Maps

You can use the templates on pages 63–64 to create road maps to go along with picture books of your choice. Simply copy the template, fill in the title and author information, and add art and text related to the book, modeling the map after those found in this resource. You might also invite students to use the templates to make reading response road maps to go along with some of their own favorite picture books.

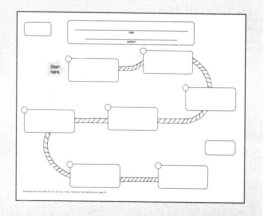

Meeting the Common Core State Standards

The activities in this book will help you meet your specific state language arts standards as well as those recommended by the Common Core State Standards Initiative (CCSSI). These materials address the following standards for students in grades K–2. For more information, visit the CCSSI website at www.corestandards.org.

Reading Standards for Literature

Key Ideas and Details

- RL.K.1, RL.1.1, RL.2.1. Ask and answer questions about key details in a text.
- RL.K.2, RL.1.2, RL.2.2. Retell stories, including key details, and demonstrate understanding of their central message or lesson.
- RL.K.3, RL.1.3, RL.2.3. Describe characters, settings, and major events in a story, using key details.

Craft and Structure

- RL.K.5, RL.1.5. Explain major differences between books that tell stories and books that give information.
- RL.2.5. Describe the overall structure of a story, including describing how the beginning introduces the story and the ending concludes the action.

Integration of Knowledge and Ideas
GRADE K

- RL.K.7, RL.1.7, RL.2.7. Use information gained from the illustrations and words in a text to describe and demonstrate understanding of its characters, setting, or plot.

Range of Reading and Level of Text Complexity

- RL.K.10. Actively engage in group reading activities with purpose and understanding.
- RL.1.10, RL.2.10. By the end of year, read and comprehend literature appropriately complex for grade level, with scaffolding as needed.

Reading Standards for Informational Text

Key Ideas and Details

- RI.K.1, RI.1.1, RI.2.1. Ask and answer such questions to demonstrate understanding of key details in a text.
- RI.K.2, RI.1.2, RI.2.2. Identify the main topic and retell key details of a text.
- RI.K.3, RI.1.3, RI.2.3. Describe the connection between two individuals, events, ideas, or pieces of information in a text.

Craft and Structure

- RI.K.4, RI.1.4, RI.2.4. Determine the meaning of words and phrases in a text.
- RI.K.6, RI.1.6, RI.2.6. Identify the main purpose of a text, including what the author wants to answer, explain, or describe.

Integration of Knowledge and Ideas

- RI.K.7, RI.1.7, RI.2.7. Use the illustrations and details in a text to describe its key ideas.

Range of Reading and Level of Text Complexity

- RI.K.10. Actively engage in group reading activities with purpose and understanding.
- RI.1.10, RI.2.10. By the end of year, read and comprehend informational texts appropriately complex for grade level, with scaffolding as needed.

Reading Standards: Foundational Skills

Fluency

- RF.K.4, RF.1.4, RF.2.4. Read with sufficient accuracy and fluency to support comprehension.
- RF.1.4a, RF2.4a. Read grade-level text with purpose and understanding.
- RF.1.4b, RF2.4b. Read grade-level text orally with accuracy, appropriate rate, and expression.
- RF.1.4c, RF2.4c. Use context to confirm or self-correct word recognition and understanding, rereading as necessary.

Speaking & Listening

Comprehension and Collaboration

- SL.K.1, SL.1.1, SL.2.1. Participate in collaborative conversations about grade-level texts with peers and adults in small and larger groups.
- SL.K.2, SL.1.2, SL.2.2. Ask and answer questions about key details in a text read aloud.
- SL.1.3, SL.2.3. Ask and answer questions about what a speaker says in order to clarify comprehension, gather additional information, or deepen understanding of a topic or issue.

Presentation of Knowledge and Ideas

- SL.K.4, SL.1.4, SL.2.4. Tell a story, recount an experience, or describe people, places, things, and events with relevant details, expressing ideas and feelings clearly.

Language

Vocabulary Acquisition and Use

- L.K.4, L.1.4, L.2.4. Determine or clarify the meaning of unknown and multiple-meaning words and phrases based on grade-level reading and content.
- L.K.5, L.1.5, L.2.5. Demonstrate understanding of word relationships and nuances in word meanings.

Growing Vegetable Soup
by Lois Ehlert

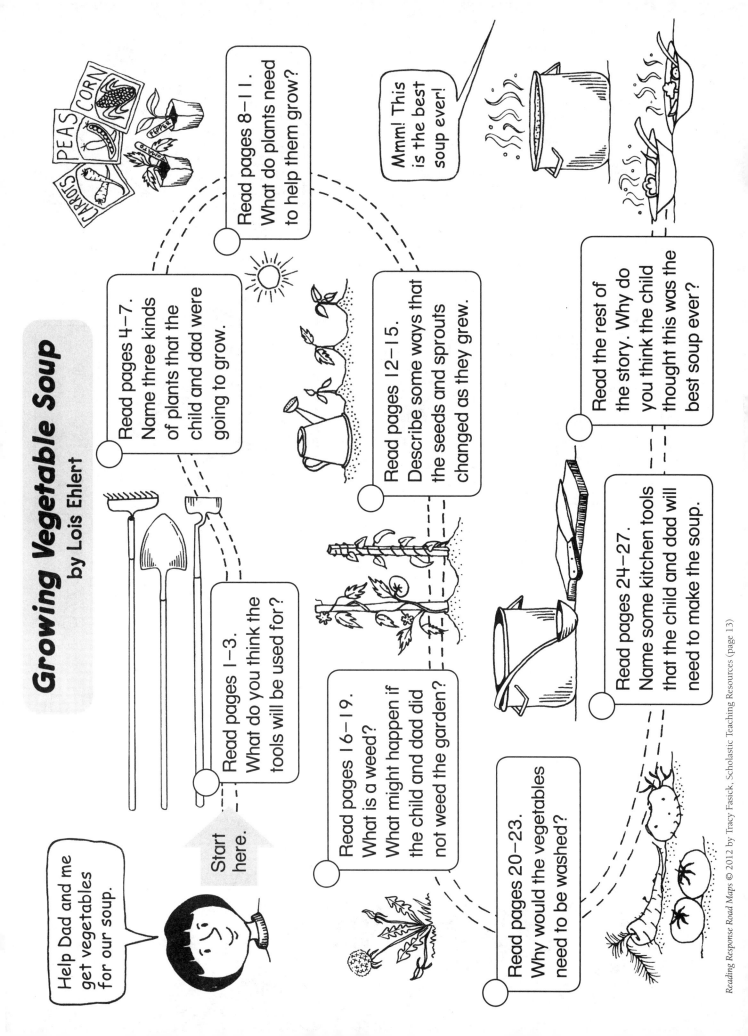

Help Dad and me get vegetables for our soup.

Start here.

Read pages 1–3. What do you think the tools will be used for?

Read pages 4–7. Name three kinds of plants that the child and dad were going to grow.

Read pages 8–11. What do plants need to help them grow?

Read pages 12–15. Describe some ways that the seeds and sprouts changed as they grew.

Read pages 16–19. What is a weed? What might happen if the child and dad did not weed the garden?

Read pages 20–23. Why would the vegetables need to be washed?

Read pages 24–27. Name some kitchen tools that the child and dad will need to make the soup.

Read the rest of the story. Why do you think the child thought this was the best soup ever?

Mmm! This is the best soup ever!

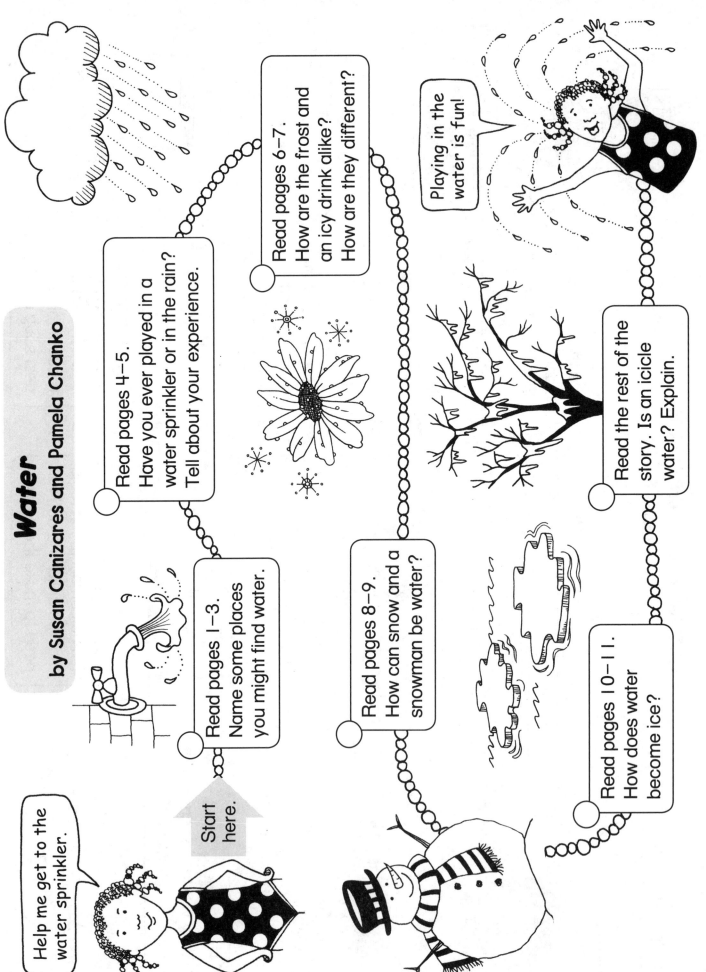

Water
by Susan Canizares and Pamela Chanko

Read pages 4–5. Have you ever played in a water sprinkler or in the rain? Tell about your experience.

Read pages 6–7. How are the frost and an icy drink alike? How are they different?

Playing in the water is fun!

Read the rest of the story. Is an icicle water? Explain.

Read pages 1–3. Name some places you might find water.

Read pages 8–9. How can snow and a snowman be water?

Read pages 10–11. How does water become ice?

Help me get to the water sprinkler.

Start here.

Brown Bear, Brown Bear, What Do You See?
by Bill Martin Jr and Eric Carle

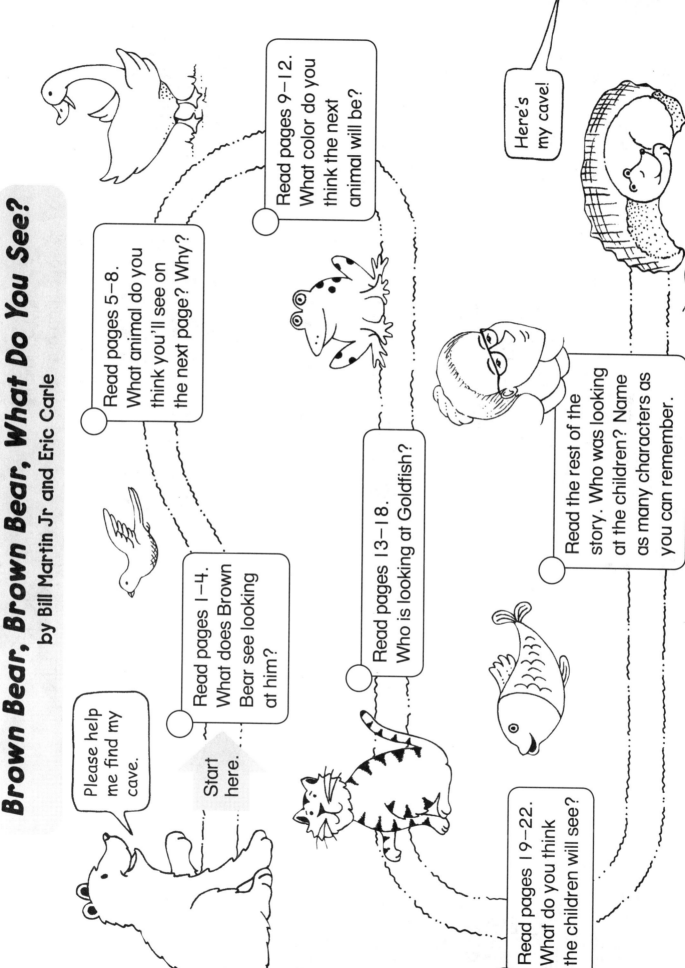

Here's my cave!

Read pages 9–12. What color do you think the next animal will be?

Read pages 5–8. What animal do you think you'll see on the next page? Why?

Read the rest of the story. Who was looking at the children? Name as many characters as you can remember.

Read pages 13–18. Who is looking at Goldfish?

Please help me find my cave.

Read pages 1–4. What does Brown Bear see looking at him?

Start here.

Read pages 19–22. What do you think the children will see?

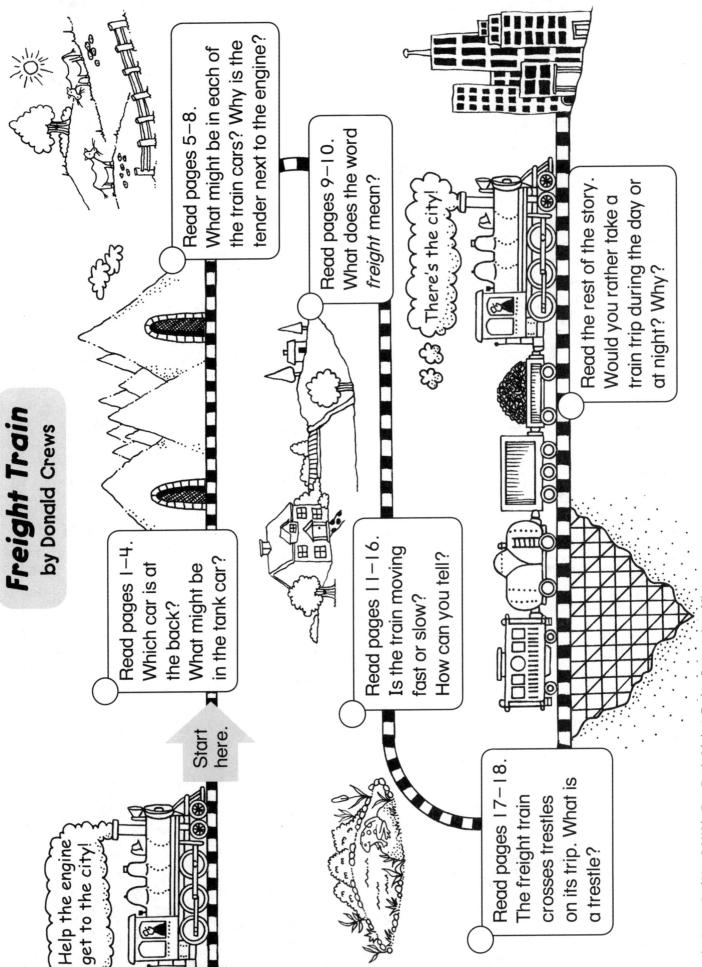

Freight Train by Donald Crews

Help the engine get to the city!

Start here.

Read pages 1–4. Which car is at the back? What might be in the tank car?

Read pages 5–8. What might be in each of the train cars? Why is the tender next to the engine?

Read pages 9–10. What does the word *freight* mean?

Read pages 11–16. Is the train moving fast or slow? How can you tell?

Read pages 17–18. The freight train crosses trestles on its trip. What is a trestle?

There's the city!

Read the rest of the story. Would you rather take a train trip during the day or at night? Why?

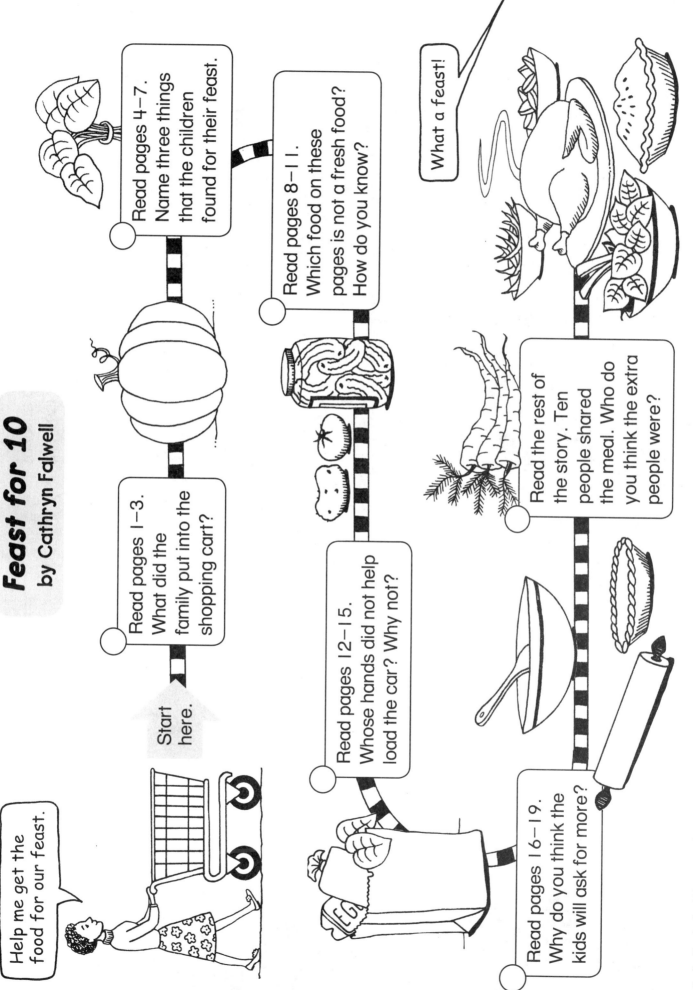

Feast for 10
by Cathryn Falwell

Help me get the food for our feast.

Start here.

Read pages 1–3. What did the family put into the shopping cart?

Read pages 4–7. Name three things that the children found for their feast.

Read pages 8–11. Which food on these pages is not a fresh food? How do you know?

Read pages 12–15. Whose hands did not help load the car? Why not?

Read pages 16–19. Why do you think the kids will ask for more?

Read the rest of the story. Ten people shared the meal. Who do you think the extra people were?

What a feast!

Cat's Colors
by Jane Cabrera

Help me find my favorite color.

Start here.

Read pages 1–2.
What does a question mark mean? Which color do you think is Cat's favorite?

Read pages 3–6.
Where did Cat see the colors green and pink?

Read pages 7–10.
What does *swoop* mean? What does *snooze* mean? Where does Cat snooze?

Read pages 11–16.
What is yellow and brown to Cat? Why would yarn get tangled in Cat's claws?

Read pages 17–20.
What colors are on these pages? What is each color to Cat?

Read the rest of the story. Why does Cat like orange the best? What is your favorite color? Why?

I'm your favorite color!

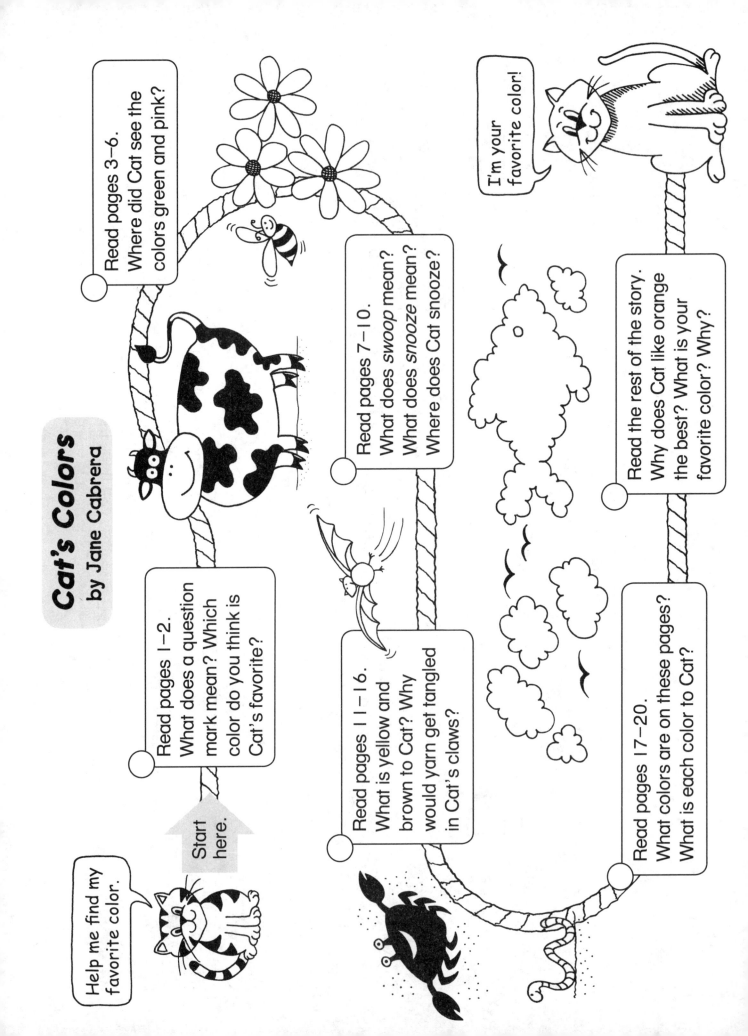

Mrs. Wishy-Washy
by Joy Cowley

Help Mrs. Wishy-Washy get bath supplies for the animals.

Bath time!

Read pages 5–6. What did the duck do in the mud?

Read pages 3–4. Why do you think the pig thought the mud was lovely?

Read pages 7–8. Why did Mrs. Wishy-Washy scream?

Read the rest of the story. What do you think Mrs. Wishy-Washy will do when she comes back outside?

Start here.

Read pages 1–2. What did the cow do?

Read pages 9–12. In what order did the animals go into the tub?

Read pages 13–14. What do you think the animals will do next?

BUBBLE BATH for Animals — Rub-A-Dub

Cookie's Week
by Cindy Ward

Help me find my bed.

Start here.

Read pages 1–3.
Where did the water come from?

Read pages 4–7.
What is a windowsill?
Why would plants be on a windowsill?

Read pages 8–11.
Where in the house do you think the garbage can was? Explain your answer.

Read pages 12–15.
What happened when Cookie got stuck in the kitchen drawer?

Read pages 16–19.
Why might Cookie's family want to keep the closet door closed?

Read the rest of the story.
What happened when Cookie climbed the curtain? Do you think Cookie will rest on Sunday? Why or why not?

Here's my bed!
Should I rest?

Pumpkin Pumpkin
by Jeanne Titherington

Please help me get to my jack-o'-lantern.

Start here.

Read pages 4–5. Why do you think Jamie planted the pumpkin seed?

Read pages 6–7. What is a sprout?

Read pages 8–9. What grew from the sprout?

Read pages 10–11. Do you think Jamie took good care of his pumpkin plant? Why or why not?

Read pages 12–13. What color was the baby pumpkin?

Read pages 14–19. How can you tell that time has passed on these pages?

Read the rest of the story. Why did Jamie save seeds from his pumpkin?

Boo!

Buzz, Said the Bee
by Wendy Cheyette Lewison

Buzz! Help me get to the flower!

Start here.

Read pages 1–3. What did the bee do when the duck said, "Scat?"

Read pages 4–7. What two things did the duck do next?

Read pages 8–11. What was the pig's problem?

Buzz! Perfect!

Read pages 12–15. Which animals were on the cow?

Read pages 16–17. Why do you think the cow began to weep?

Read the rest of the story. Why did the animals run away?

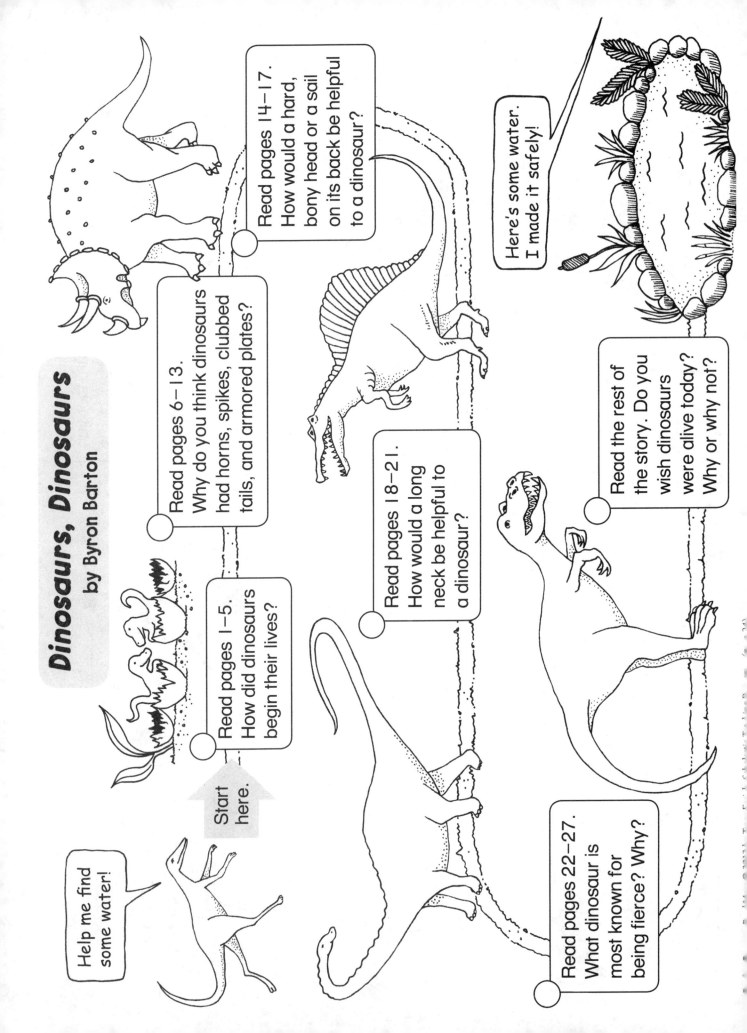

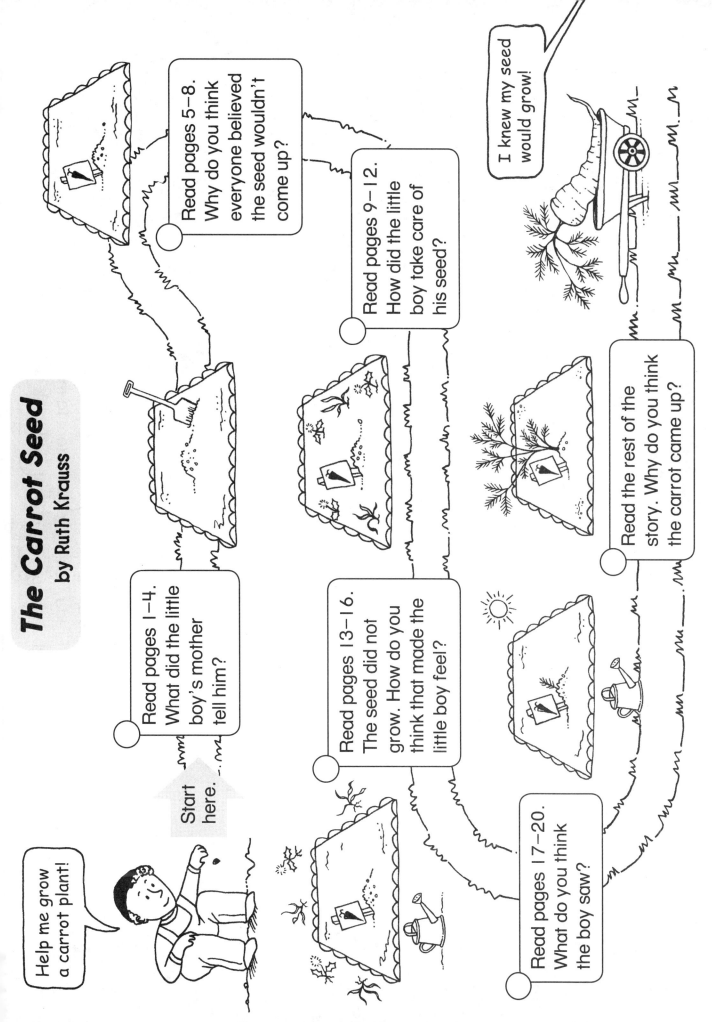

The Carrot Seed
by Ruth Krauss

Help me grow a carrot plant!

Start here.

Read pages 1–4. What did the little boy's mother tell him?

Read pages 5–8. Why do you think everyone believed the seed wouldn't come up?

Read pages 9–12. How did the little boy take care of his seed?

Read pages 13–16. The seed did not grow. How do you think that made the little boy feel?

Read pages 17–20. What do you think the boy saw?

Read the rest of the story. Why do you think the carrot came up?

I knew my seed would grow!

More Spaghetti, I Say!
by Rita Golden Gelman

Help me find Minnie.

Start here.

Read pages 1–4. Why wouldn't Minnie play with Freddy?

Read pages 5–6. Why did Freddy think it was a good time for Minnie to play? Do you think Minnie will play with him?

Read pages 7–12. Name five ways Minnie liked her spaghetti. Would you like spaghetti any of these ways?

Hi, Freddy! Have some spaghetti!

Read pages 13–16. Where did Minnie eat spaghetti? Name three things she did in spaghetti.

Read pages 17–20. How do you think Freddy felt about Minnie's love for spaghetti? Why might he have felt this way?

Read pages 21–24. Why did Freddy take the spaghetti away?

Read the rest of the story. How did Freddy change from the beginning of the story to the end? Why do you think he changed?

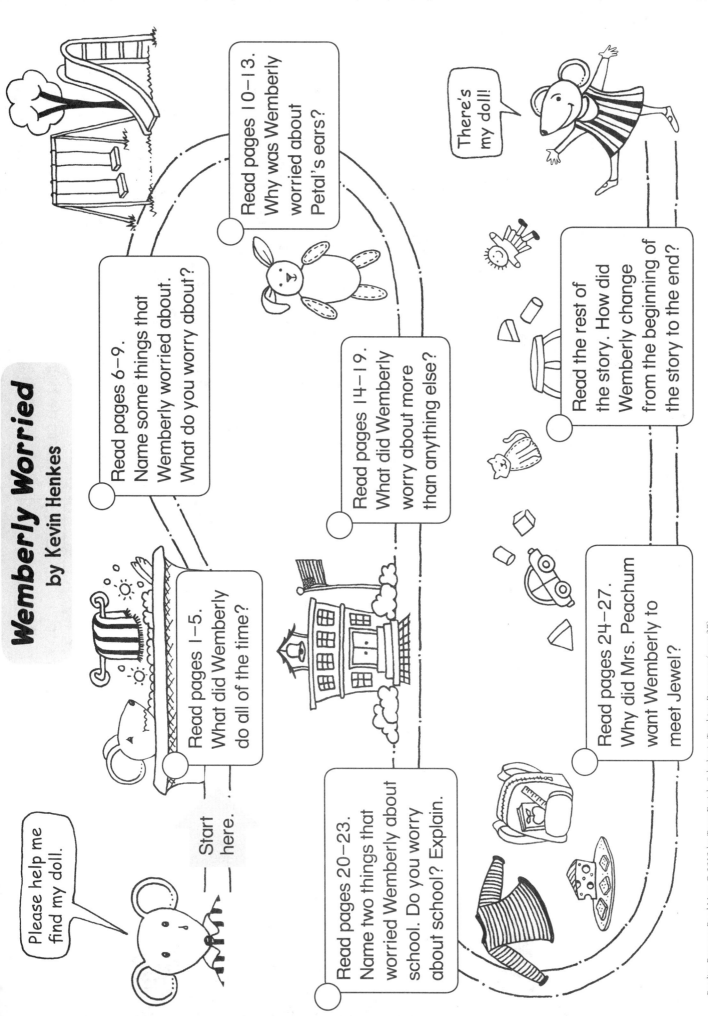

Wemberly Worried
by Kevin Henkes

Please help me find my doll.

Start here.

Read pages 1–5. What did Wemberly do all of the time?

Read pages 6–9. Name some things that Wemberly worried about. What do you worry about?

Read pages 10–13. Why was Wemberly worried about Petal's ears?

There's my doll!

Read pages 14–19. What did Wemberly worry about more than anything else?

Read the rest of the story. How did Wemberly change from the beginning of the story to the end?

Read pages 20–23. Name two things that worried Wemberly about school. Do you worry about school? Explain.

Read pages 24–27. Why did Mrs. Peachum want Wemberly to meet Jewel?

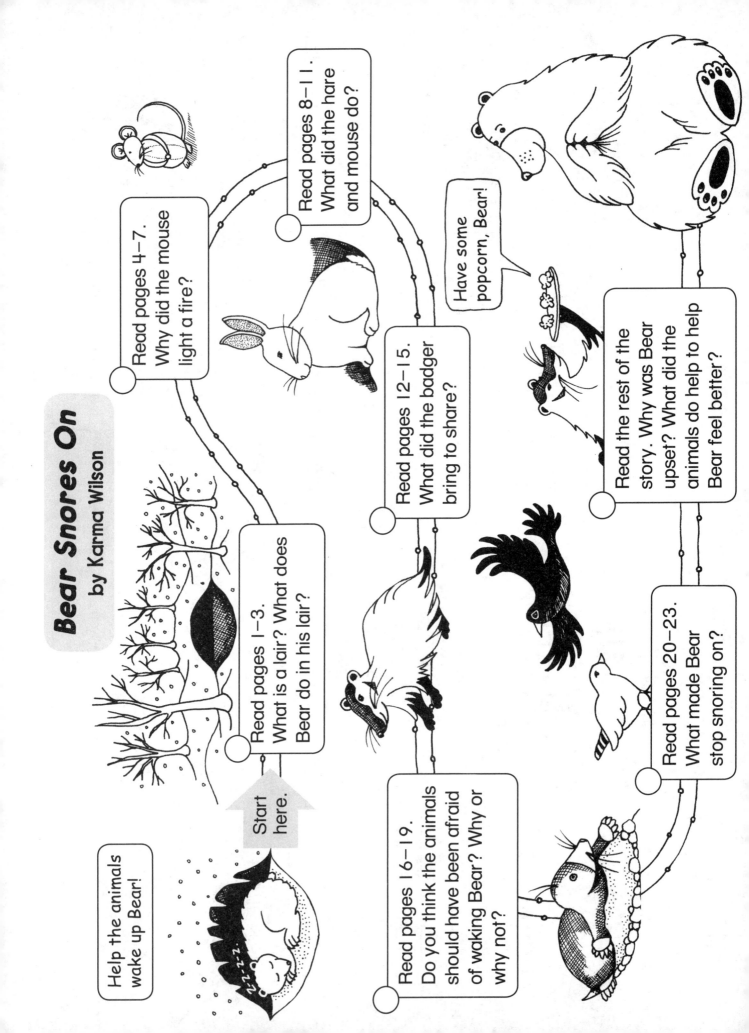

Bear Snores On
by Karma Wilson

Help the animals wake up Bear!

Start here.

Read pages 1–3. What is a lair? What does Bear do in his lair?

Read pages 4–7. Why did the mouse light a fire?

Read pages 8–11. What did the hare and mouse do?

Read pages 12–15. What did the badger bring to share?

Have some popcorn, Bear!

Read pages 16–19. Do you think the animals should have been afraid of waking Bear? Why or why not?

Read pages 20–23. What made Bear stop snoring on?

Read the rest of the story. Why was Bear upset? What did the animals do help to help Bear feel better?

Just My Friend and Me
by Mercer Mayer

Help me find my friend!

Start here.

Read pages 1–4. Why did Little Critter want to have a friend over?

Read pages 5–8. What three things did Little Critter and his friend do together?

Read pages 9–12. Why do you think Little Critter's friend liked to hit the ball, but not chase it?

Hi, friend!

Read pages 13–16. What do you think will happen to Little Critter's friend on the bike?

Read pages 17–20. Why did Little Critter and his friend cry when they got their cuts and bruises fixed?

Read the rest of the story. Why do you think Little Critter liked to be all alone sometimes?

First Aid Kit

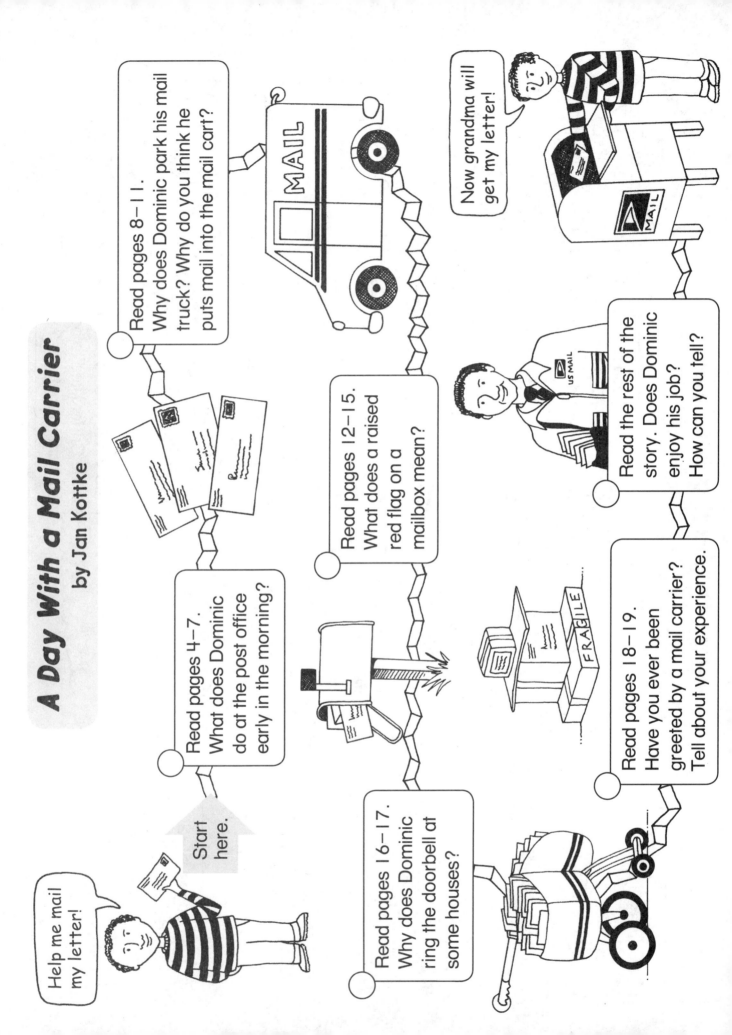

A Day With a Mail Carrier
by Jan Kottke

Help me mail my letter!

Start here.

Read pages 4–7. What does Dominic do at the post office early in the morning?

Read pages 8–11. Why does Dominic park his mail truck? Why do you think he puts mail into the mail cart?

Read pages 12–15. What does a raised red flag on a mailbox mean?

Read pages 16–17. Why does Dominic ring the doorbell at some houses?

Read pages 18–19. Have you ever been greeted by a mail carrier? Tell about your experience.

Read the rest of the story. Does Dominic enjoy his job? How can you tell?

Now grandma will get my letter!

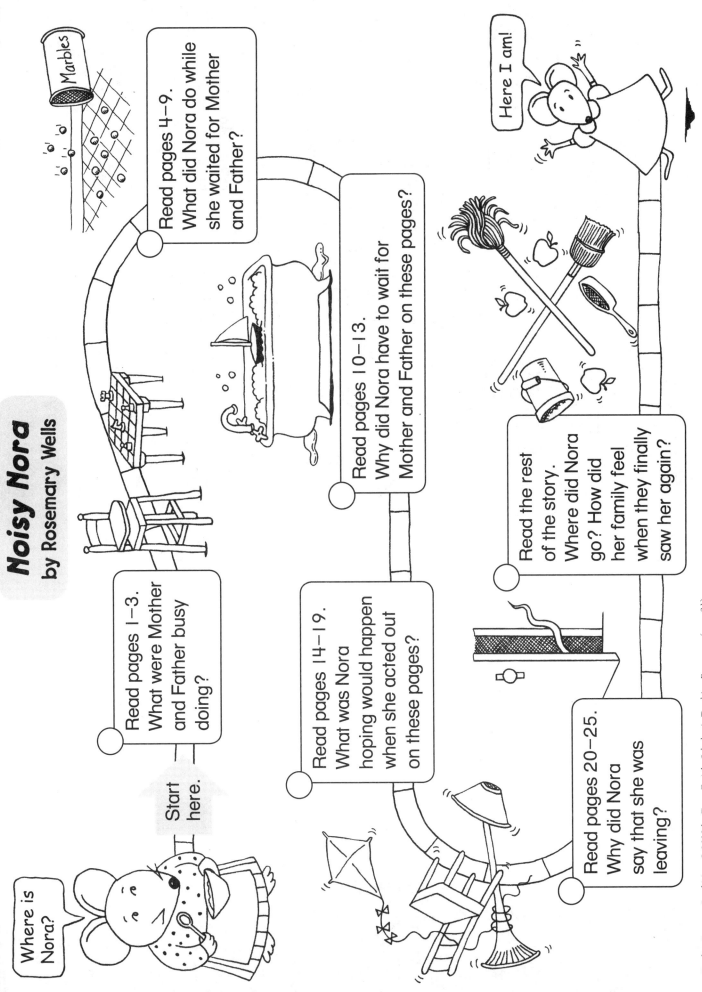

Noisy Nora
by Rosemary Wells

Marbles

Read pages 4–9. What did Nora do while she waited for Mother and Father?

Read pages 1–3. What were Mother and Father busy doing?

Start here.

Read pages 10–13. Why did Nora have to wait for Mother and Father on these pages?

Read pages 14–19. What was Nora hoping would happen when she acted out on these pages?

Read the rest of the story. Where did Nora go? How did her family feel when they finally saw her again?

Read pages 20–25. Why did Nora say that she was leaving?

Here I am!

Where is Nora?

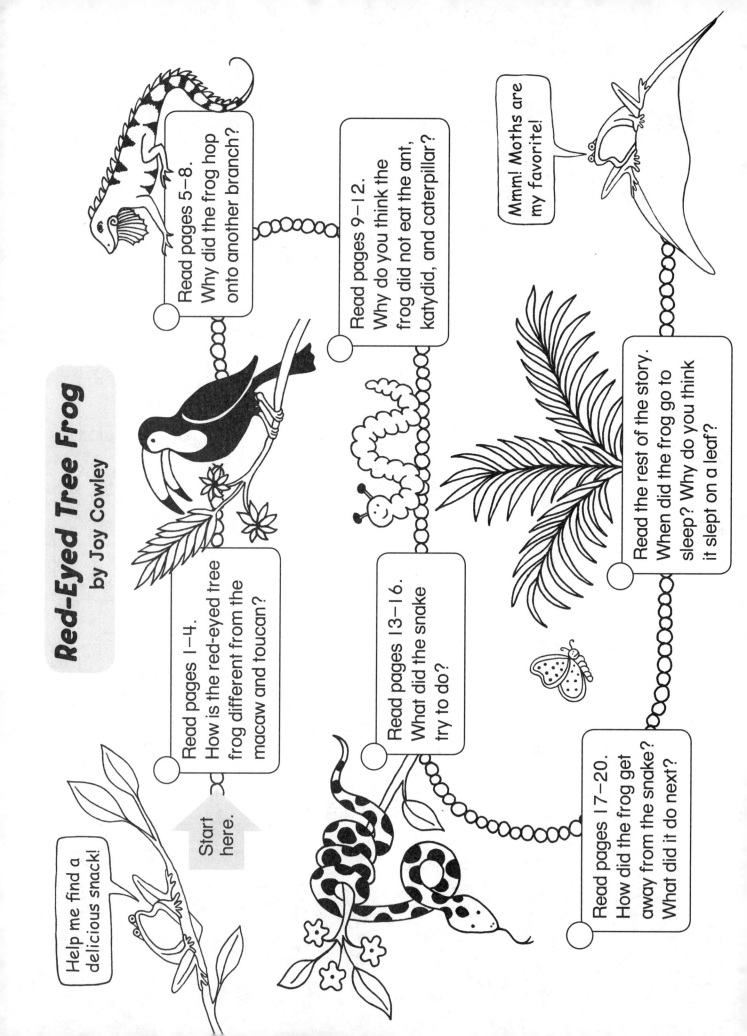

Red-Eyed Tree Frog
by Joy Cowley

Help me find a delicious snack!

Start here.

Read pages 1–4.
How is the red-eyed tree frog different from the macaw and toucan?

Read pages 5–8.
Why did the frog hop onto another branch?

Read pages 9–12.
Why do you think the frog did not eat the ant, katydid, and caterpillar?

Read pages 13–16.
What did the snake try to do?

Read pages 17–20.
How did the frog get away from the snake? What did it do next?

Read the rest of the story. When did the frog go to sleep? Why do you think it slept on a leaf?

Mmm! Moths are my favorite!

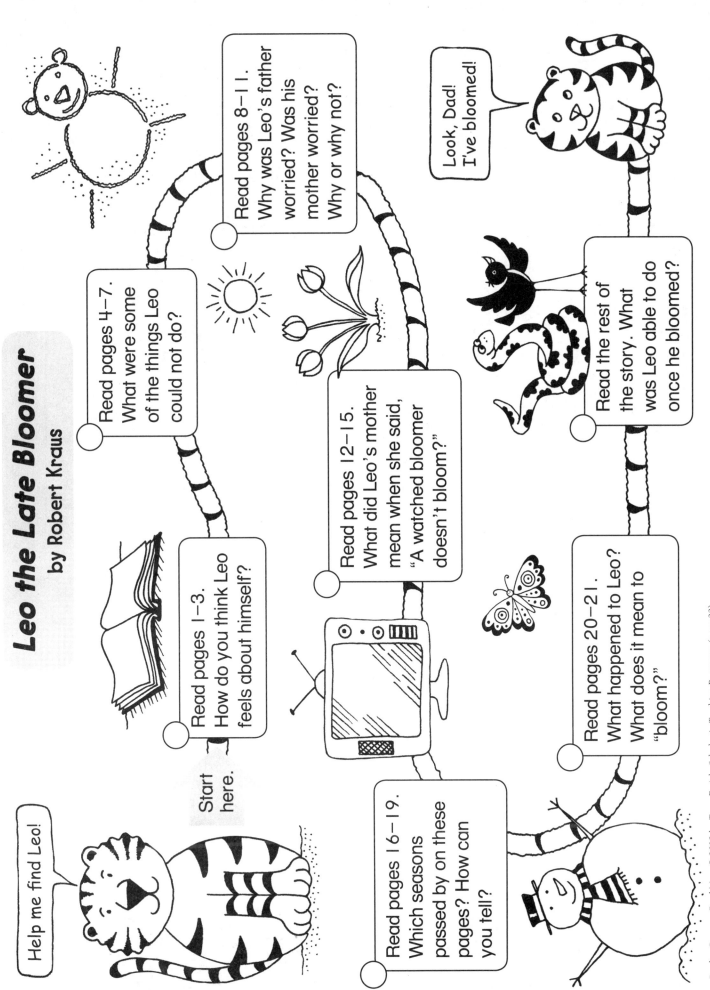

Leo the Late Bloomer
by Robert Kraus

Help me find Leo!

Read pages 1–3. How do you think Leo feels about himself?

Start here.

Read pages 4–7. What were some of the things Leo could not do?

Read pages 8–11. Why was Leo's father worried? Was his mother worried? Why or why not?

Look, Dad! I've bloomed!

Read pages 12–15. What did Leo's mother mean when she said, "A watched bloomer doesn't bloom?"

Read pages 16–19. Which seasons passed by on these pages? How can you tell?

Read pages 20–21. What happened to Leo? What does it mean to "bloom?"

Read the rest of the story. What was Leo able to do once he bloomed?

The Little Old Lady Who Was Not Afraid of Anything
by Linda Williams

Help me make a scarecrow!

Read pages 7–10. What sounds do you think the little old lady heard behind her?

Read pages 11–12. Was the little old lady afraid of the shirt? How do you know?

BOO!

Read pages 1–6. Do you think the little old lady was afraid of the shoes? Why or why not?

Start here.

Read pages 13–14. Why did the little old lady walk just a little bit faster?

Read the rest of the story. What was the little old lady's plan?

Read pages 15–16. What do you think the head will do?

Read pages 17–22. Do you think the little old lady was brave to open the door? Why or why not?

The Very Hungry Caterpillar
by Eric Carle

I'm hungry! Please help me find something to eat.

Start here.

Read pages 1–2. What do you think is inside the egg?

Read pages 3–4. What popped out of the egg on Sunday?

Read pages 5–6. What did the caterpillar eat on Monday?

Read pages 7–10. Why do you think the caterpillar was so hungry?

Read pages 11–14. What did the caterpillar eat on each day from Monday through Friday?

Read pages 15–16. Why did the caterpillar have a stomachache on Saturday night?

Read the rest of the story. Describe what happened to the caterpillar on these pages.

Look! I'm a beautiful butterfly!

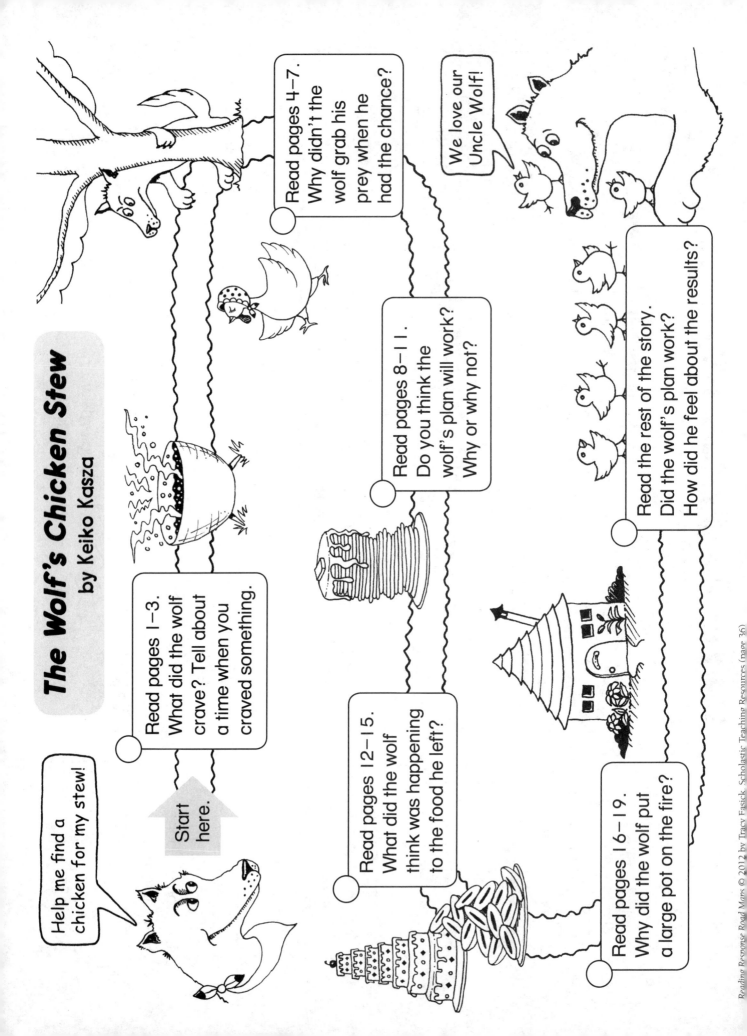

The Wolf's Chicken Stew
by Keiko Kasza

Help me find a chicken for my stew!

Start here.

Read pages 1–3. What did the wolf crave? Tell about a time when you craved something.

Read pages 4–7. Why didn't the wolf grab his prey when he had the chance?

We love our Uncle Wolf!

Read pages 8–11. Do you think the wolf's plan will work? Why or why not?

Read the rest of the story. Did the wolf's plan work? How did he feel about the results?

Read pages 12–15. What did the wolf think was happening to the food he left?

Read pages 16–19. Why did the wolf put a large pot on the fire?

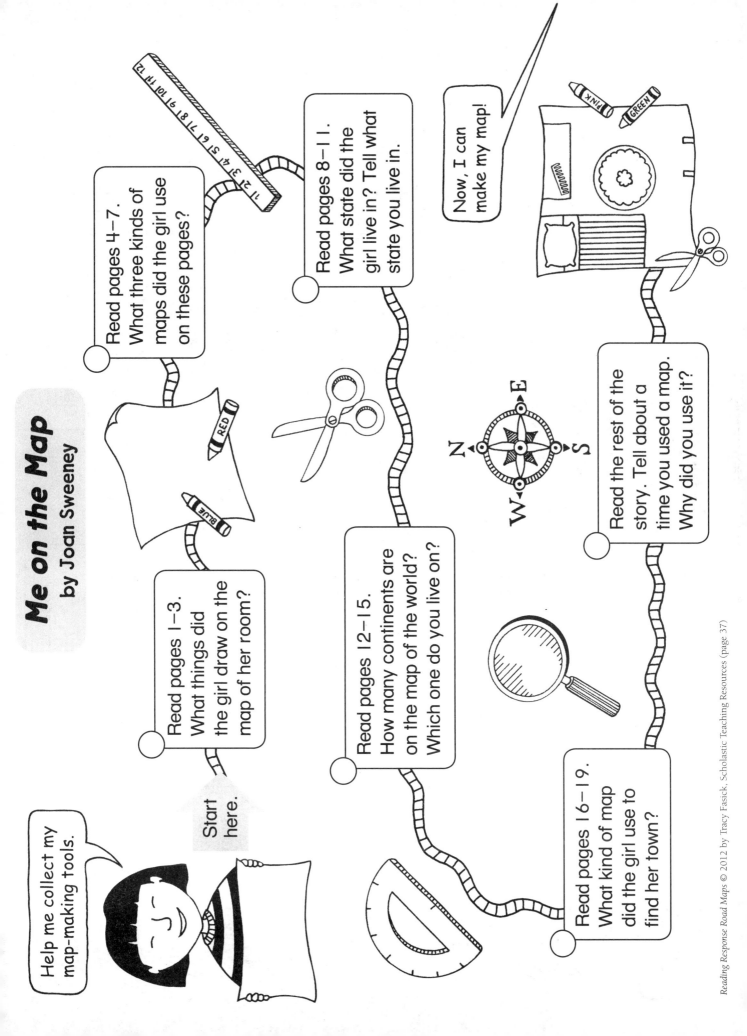

Me on the Map
by Joan Sweeney

Help me collect my map-making tools.

Start here.

Read pages 1–3. What things did the girl draw on the map of her room?

Read pages 4–7. What three kinds of maps did the girl use on these pages?

Read pages 8–11. What state did the girl live in? Tell what state you live in.

Now, I can make my map!

Read pages 12–15. How many continents are on the map of the world? Which one do you live on?

Read pages 16–19. What kind of map did the girl use to find her town?

Read the rest of the story. Tell about a time you used a map. Why did you use it?

Bark, George
by Jules Feiffer

Where is my bark?

Start here.

Read pages 1–3. What sound did George make?

Read pages 4–7. How did George's mom feel about the sounds he made?

Read pages 8–9. Why do you think George didn't bark?

ARF!

Read the rest of the story. Why do you think George said hello?

Home

Read pages 10–13. Where was the cat? How do you think it got there?

Vet's Office

Read pages 14–19. What do you think will happen next?

Read pages 20–25. How did George's mother feel when he barked? What did she do?

There's Something in My Attic
by Mercer Mayer

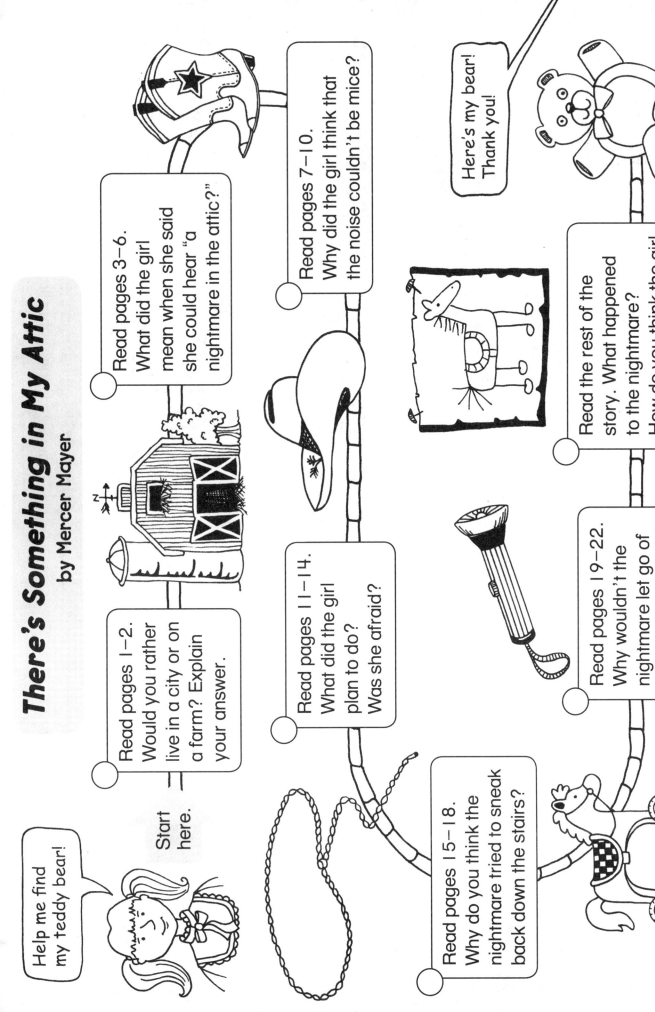

Help me find my teddy bear!

Start here.

Read pages 1–2. Would you rather live in a city or on a farm? Explain your answer.

Read pages 3–6. What did the girl mean when she said she could hear "a nightmare in the attic?"

Read pages 7–10. Why did the girl think that the noise couldn't be mice?

Read pages 11–14. What did the girl plan to do? Was she afraid?

Read pages 15–18. Why do you think the nightmare tried to sneak back down the stairs?

Read pages 19–22. Why wouldn't the nightmare let go of the girl's bear?

Read the rest of the story. What happened to the nightmare? How do you think the girl will get her bear back?

Here's my bear! Thank you!

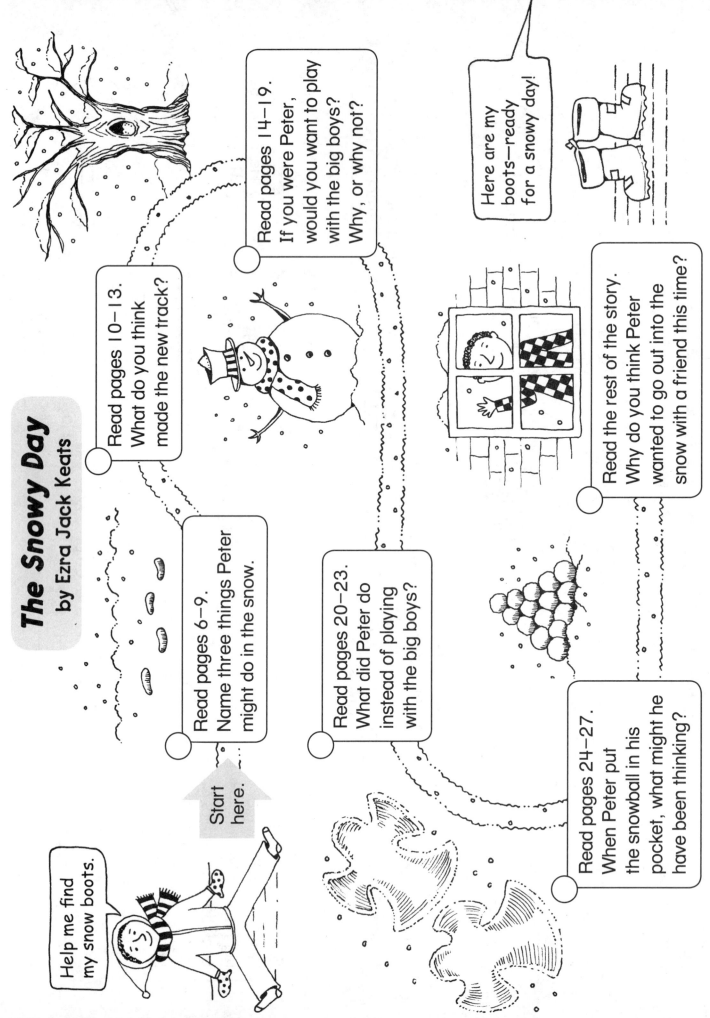

The Snowy Day
by Ezra Jack Keats

Help me find my snow boots.

Start here.

Read pages 6–9. Name three things Peter might do in the snow.

Read pages 10–13. What do you think made the new track?

Read pages 14–19. If you were Peter, would you want to play with the big boys? Why, or why not?

Here are my boots—ready for a snowy day!

Read pages 20–23. What did Peter do instead of playing with the big boys?

Read pages 24–27. When Peter put the snowball in his pocket, what might he have been thinking?

Read the rest of the story. Why do you think Peter wanted to go out into the snow with a friend this time?

Clifford's Thanksgiving Visit
by Norman Bridwell

Help Clifford find his mom.

Read pages 4–7. Who did Clifford set out to see on Thanksgiving? Why did he decide to do this?

Read pages 8–11. What happened when Clifford crossed the bridge? How did he get wet?

It's my baby, Clifford!

Read the rest of the story. Why did Clifford hurry home? Why would he be happy to be home again?

Start here.

Read pages 1–3. Why didn't Clifford go with Emily Elizabeth to visit her grandma?

Read pages 12–17. Why did Clifford go into the tunnel? What happened to him there?

Read pages 26–27. How were Clifford and his mom different? How were they the same?

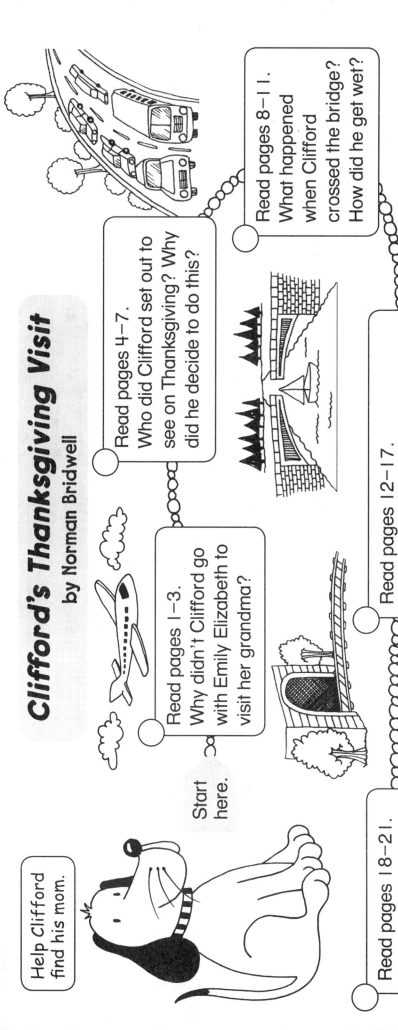

Read pages 18–21. How did Clifford find his old neighborhood?

Read pages 22–25. How do you think Clifford wound up playing in the football game?

Reading Response Road Maps © 2012 by Tracy Fasick, Scholastic Teaching Resources (page 41)

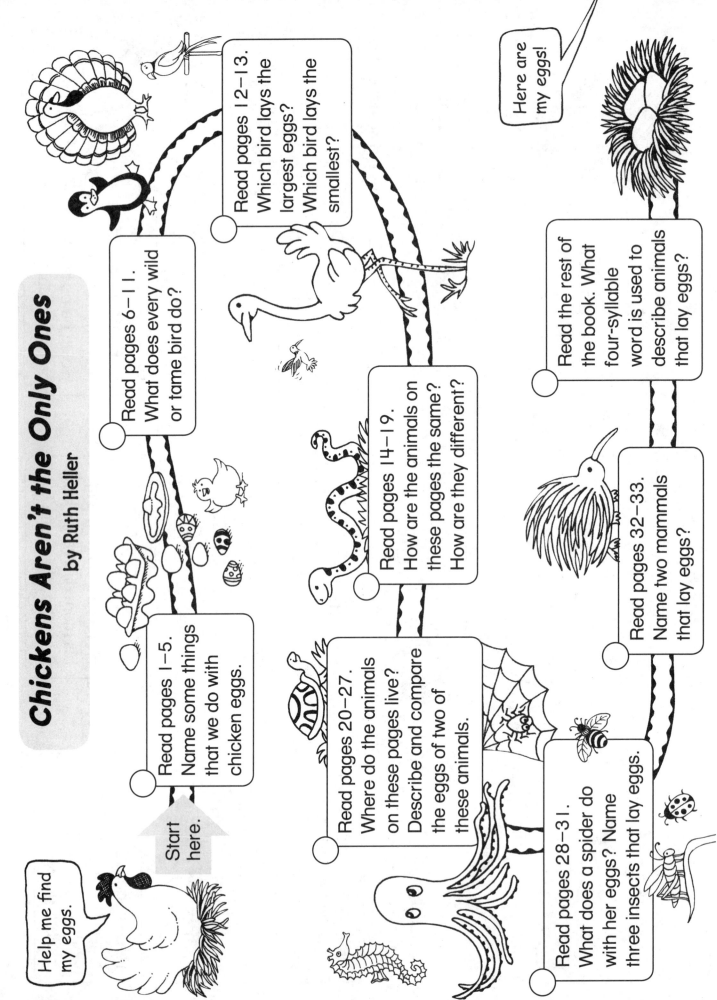

Chickens Aren't the Only Ones
by Ruth Heller

Help me find my eggs.

Start here.

Read pages 1–5. Name some things that we do with chicken eggs.

Read pages 6–11. What does every wild or tame bird do?

Read pages 12–13. Which bird lays the largest eggs? Which bird lays the smallest?

Read pages 14–19. How are the animals on these pages the same? How are they different?

Read pages 20–27. Where do the animals on these pages live? Describe and compare the eggs of two of these animals.

Read pages 28–31. What does a spider do with her eggs? Name three insects that lay eggs.

Read pages 32–33. Name two mammals that lay eggs?

Read the rest of the book. What four-syllable word is used to describe animals that lay eggs?

Here are my eggs!

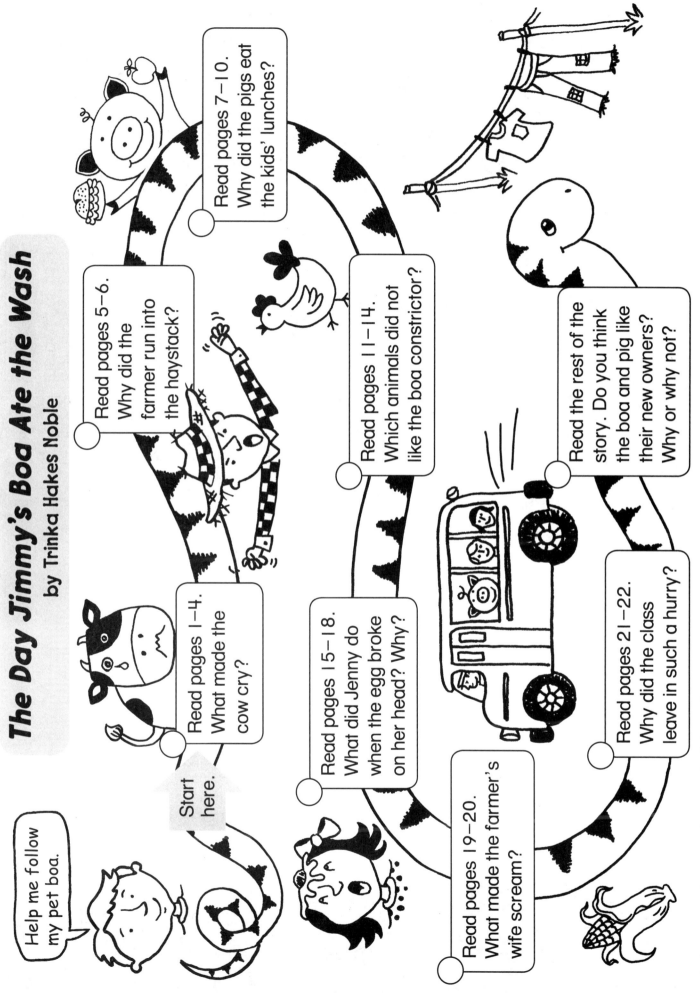

The Day Jimmy's Boa Ate the Wash
by Trinka Hakes Noble

Help me follow my pet boa.

Start here.

Read pages 1–4. What made the cow cry?

Read pages 5–6. Why did the farmer run into the haystack?

Read pages 7–10. Why did the pigs eat the kids' lunches?

Read pages 11–14. Which animals did not like the boa constrictor?

Read pages 15–18. What did Jenny do when the egg broke on her head? Why?

Read pages 19–20. What made the farmer's wife scream?

Read pages 21–22. Why did the class leave in such a hurry?

Read the rest of the story. Do you think the boa and pig like their new owners? Why or why not?

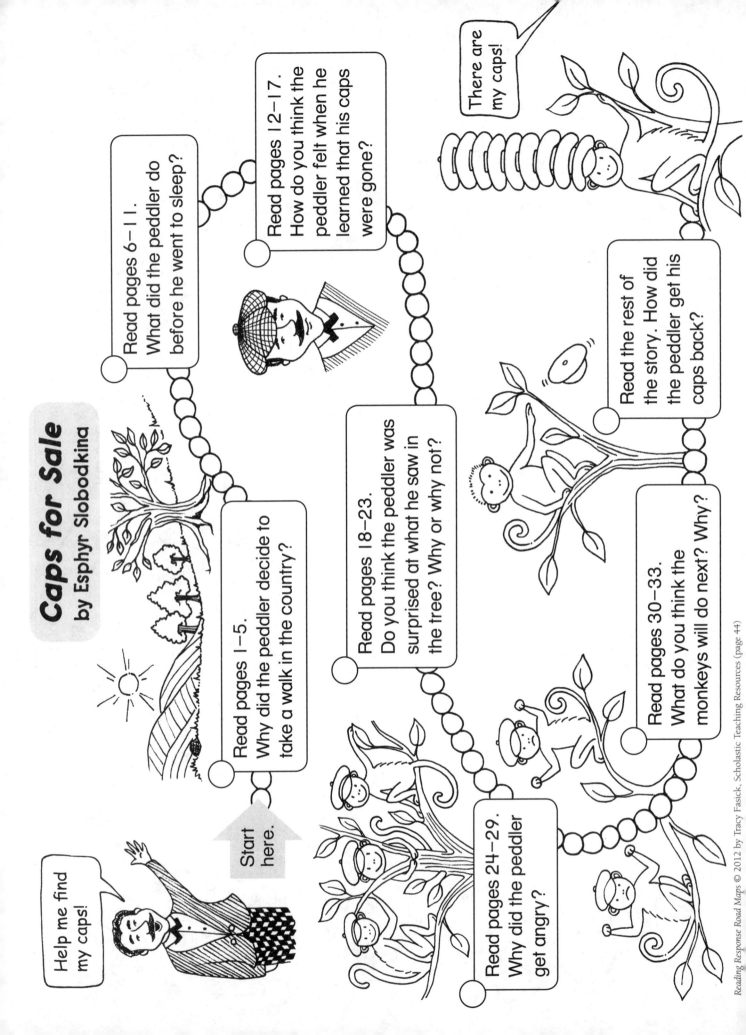

Caps for Sale
by Esphyr Slobodkina

Help me find my caps!

Start here.

Read pages 1–5. Why did the peddler decide to take a walk in the country?

Read pages 6–11. What did the peddler do before he went to sleep?

Read pages 12–17. How do you think the peddler felt when he learned that his caps were gone?

There are my caps!

Read pages 18–23. Do you think the peddler was surprised at what he saw in the tree? Why or why not?

Read the rest of the story. How did the peddler get his caps back?

Read pages 30–33. What do you think the monkeys will do next? Why?

Read pages 24–29. Why did the peddler get angry?

Plenty of Penguins
by Sonia W. Black

Help the penguin parent get to its baby.

Start here.

Read pages 1–4. Why do you think some penguins are big and some are small?

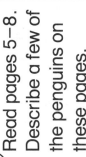

Read pages 5–8. Describe a few of the penguins on these pages.

Read pages 9–12. Name three places where penguins live.

Read pages 13–16. Why is it odd that penguins can't fly? How do they get around?

Read pages 17–20. Where do penguins get their food? How could hunting food be dangerous for penguins?

Here's my baby!

Read the rest of the story. What are penguin nests made of? How do penguins care for their eggs?

Read pages 21–24. Why do you think penguins live in groups? What are their groups called?

Click, Clack, Moo: Cows That Type
by Doreen Cronin

Where's my typewriter?

Start here.

Read pages 1–4. What is Farmer Brown's problem?

Read pages 5–8. Why couldn't Farmer Brown believe his eyes?

Dear Farmer Brown,
The barn is very cold at night. We'd like some electric blankets.
Sincerely,
The cows

Read pages 9–12. What did the cows want Farmer Brown to do for the hens?

No one will ever get this again!

Read pages 13–18. How did Farmer Brown feel about the new note from the cows? What did he do?

Read the rest of the story. Do you think the ducks did a smart thing? Why or why not?

Read pages 19–20. Why did Duck take the note to the cows?

Read pages 21–24. How did the cows respond to Farmer Brown's note?

The Mud Pony
retold by Caron Lee Cohen

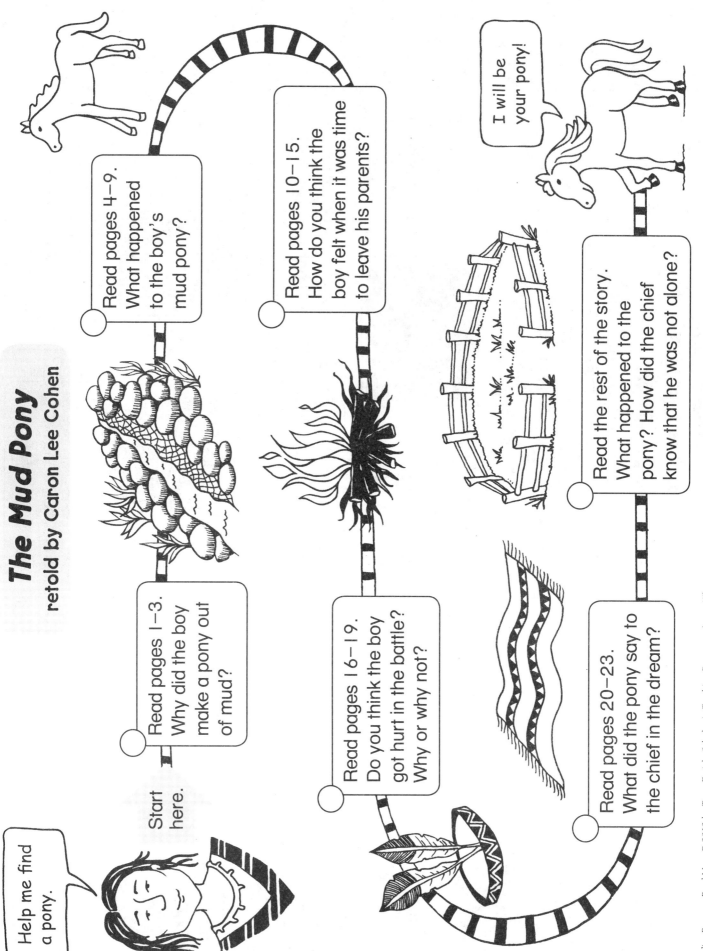

I will be your pony!

Read pages 4–9. What happened to the boy's mud pony?

Read pages 10–15. How do you think the boy felt when it was time to leave his parents?

Read pages 1–3. Why did the boy make a pony out of mud?

Read pages 16–19. Do you think the boy got hurt in the battle? Why or why not?

Read the rest of the story. What happened to the pony? How did the chief know that he was not alone?

Read pages 20–23. What did the pony say to the chief in the dream?

Start here.

Help me find a pony.

Miss Nelson Is Missing
by Harry Allard and James Marshall

Help us find our teacher.

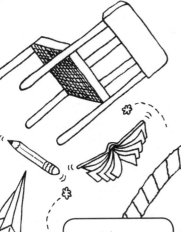

Start here.

Read pages 3–7. Why was room 207 the worst-behaved class in the school?

Read pages 8–9. Whom do you think the unpleasant voice belongs to?

Read pages 10–15. How could the children tell that Miss Viola Swamp meant business?

Hi, class. I'm back!

Read pages 16–17. Why did the kids want to find Miss Nelson?

Read the rest of the story. What was Miss Nelson's little secret?

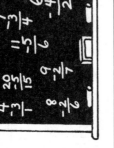

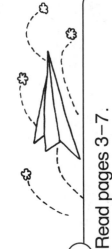

Read pages 18–19. Why do you think Miss Viola Swamp was on Miss Nelson's street?

Read pages 20–25. What unlikely things did the kids say might have happened to Miss Nelson?

Read pages 26–29. What caused the kids to change their behavior during story hour?

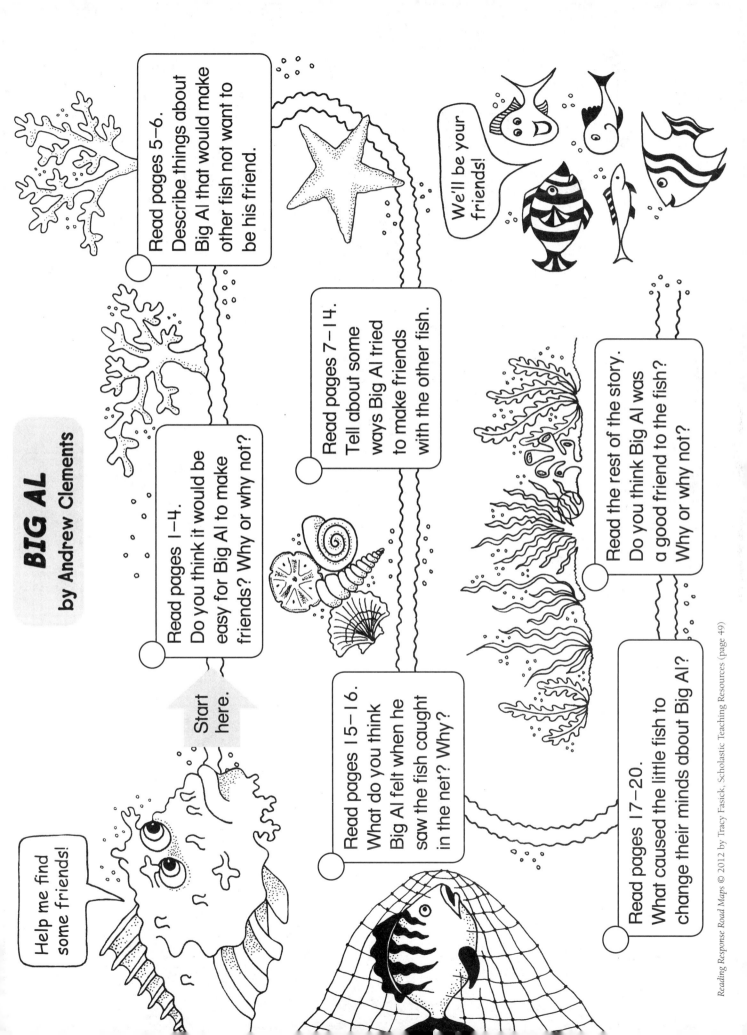

BIG AL
by Andrew Clements

Help me find some friends!

Start here.

Read pages 1–4. Do you think it would be easy for Big Al to make friends? Why or why not?

Read pages 5–6. Describe things about Big Al that would make other fish not want to be his friend.

We'll be your friends!

Read pages 7–14. Tell about some ways Big Al tried to make friends with the other fish.

Read pages 15–16. What do you think Big Al felt when he saw the fish caught in the net? Why?

Read the rest of the story. Do you think Big Al was a good friend to the fish? Why or why not?

Read pages 17–20. What caused the little fish to change their minds about Big Al?

TACKY the Penguin
by Helen Lester

Help me find some fish!

Start here.

Read pages 3–5.
Name Tacky's companions.
Who are your companions?

Read pages 6–13.
Describe three ways
Tacky was different
from his companions.

Read pages 14–15.
What do you think
the penguins felt
about the hunters?

Read pages 16–19.
As the hunters got
closer, what did Tacky's
companions do?

Read pages 20–21.
Why do you think
Tacky did not run away
from the hunters?

Read pages 22–25.
Why do you think
the hunters looked
puzzled?

Read pages 26–29.
Why did Tacky's
companions sing with him?

Read pages 30–32.
Why did Tacky's
companions think
that he was nice to
have around?

Play Ball, Amelia Bedelia
by Peggy Parish

Help me get home from the baseball game.

Start here.

Read pages 5–13. What does "gloomy faces" mean? Why did the players have gloomy faces?

Read pages 14–19. Why do you think Amelia Bedelia put on the uniform?

Read pages 20–29. What two things was Amelia Bedelia confused about on these pages?

Read pages 30–39. Why did Amelia Bedelia pick up second base?

Read pages 40–45. What did Amelia Bedelia do that made the Tornados angry?

Read pages 46–51. Why were the Grizzlies worried about Amelia Bedelia going to bat?

Read pages 52–55. Why did Amelia Bedelia scoop up all the bases? Why did she run all the way home?

Read the rest of the story. What did Amelia Bedelia do with home plate? Why?

Home is where the cookies are! Mmm!

Cactus Hotel
by Brenda Z. Guiberson

Help the owl find a home in the desert.

Start here.

Read pages 1–3. What happened to the cactus fruit seeds? How did a seed get to the paloverde tree?

Read pages 4–7. How does the paloverde tree protect the seedling?

Read pages 8–11. What desert animals get food from the saguaro cactus?

Read pages 12–15. How does the woodpecker make its nest in the cactus?

I love my new home!

Read pages 16–19. Why is the cactus hotel a good place for birds to live?

Read pages 20–21. What happens to the cactus every spring?

Read pages 22–25. Name some animals that live in the fallen cactus.

Read the rest of the story. Why do you think cactus hotels are important to the desert habitat?

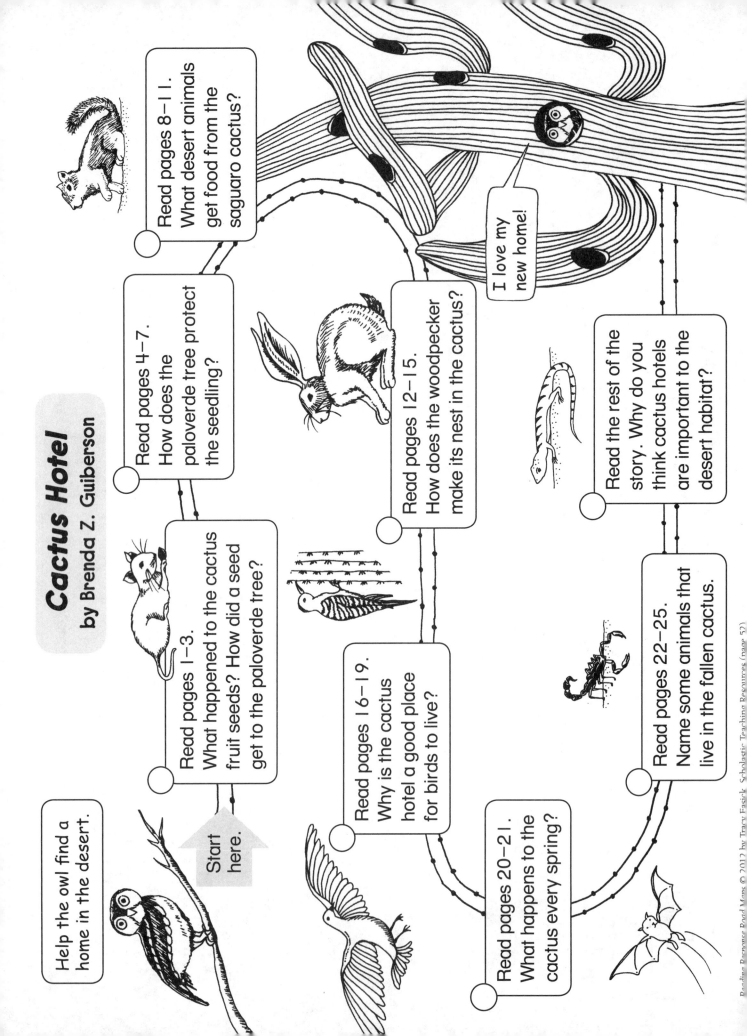

Reading Response Road Maps © 2012 by Tracy Fasick, Scholastic Teaching Resources (page 52)

Stephanie's Ponytail
by Robert Munsch

Help me find the perfect hairstyle.

Start here.

Read pages 1–2.
What did the kids say about Stephanie's ponytail?

Read pages 3–6.
Why do you think Stephanie wanted a ponytail on the side?

Read pages 7–12.
Why do you think the other kids kept copying Stephanie's ponytail?

This ponytail is perfect for me!

Read pages 13–14.
Do you think the other kids will copy Stephanie's ponytail this time? Why or why not?

Read pages 15–18.
Who wore their hair in a ponytail coming out the front? What kind of problems did they have?

Read the rest of the story.
Why did the teacher, boys, and girls shave their heads? What might Stephanie have thought when she saw them?

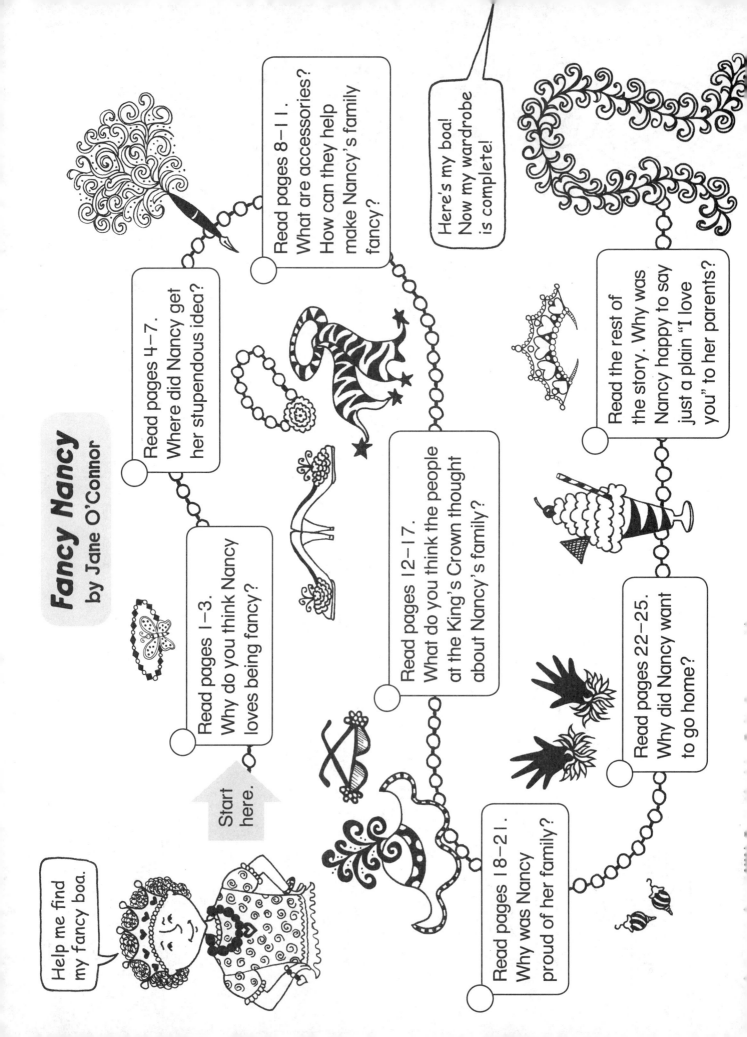

Fancy Nancy
by Jane O'Connor

Help me find my fancy boa.

Read pages 1–3. Why do you think Nancy loves being fancy?

Start here.

Read pages 4–7. Where did Nancy get her stupendous idea?

Read pages 8–11. What are accessories? How can they help make Nancy's family fancy?

Here's my boa! Now my wardrobe is complete!

Read pages 12–17. What do you think the people at the King's Crown thought about Nancy's family?

Read pages 18–21. Why was Nancy proud of her family?

Read pages 22–25. Why did Nancy want to go home?

Read the rest of the story. Why was Nancy happy to say just a plain "I love you" to her parents?

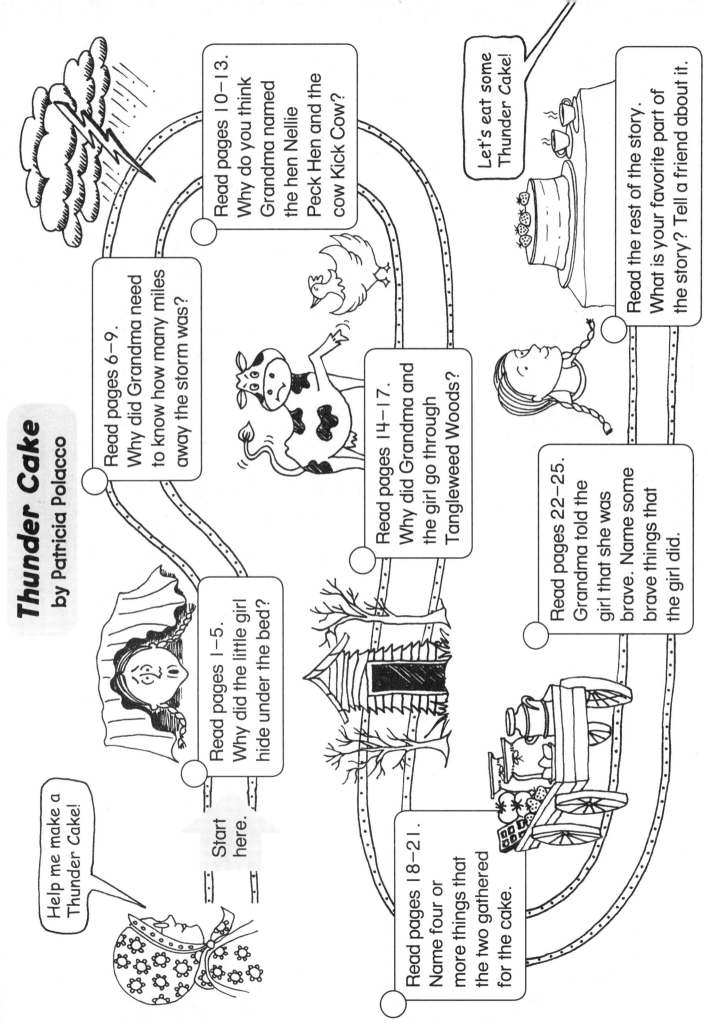

Thunder Cake
by Patricia Polacco

Help me make a Thunder Cake!

Start here.

Read pages 1–5. Why did the little girl hide under the bed?

Read pages 6–9. Why did Grandma need to know how many miles away the storm was?

Read pages 10–13. Why do you think Grandma named the hen Nellie Peck Hen and the cow Kick Cow?

Read pages 14–17. Why did Grandma and the girl go through Tangleweed Woods?

Read pages 18–21. Name four or more things that the two gathered for the cake.

Read pages 22–25. Grandma told the girl that she was brave. Name some brave things that the girl did.

Let's eat some Thunder Cake!

Read the rest of the story. What is your favorite part of the story? Tell a friend about it.

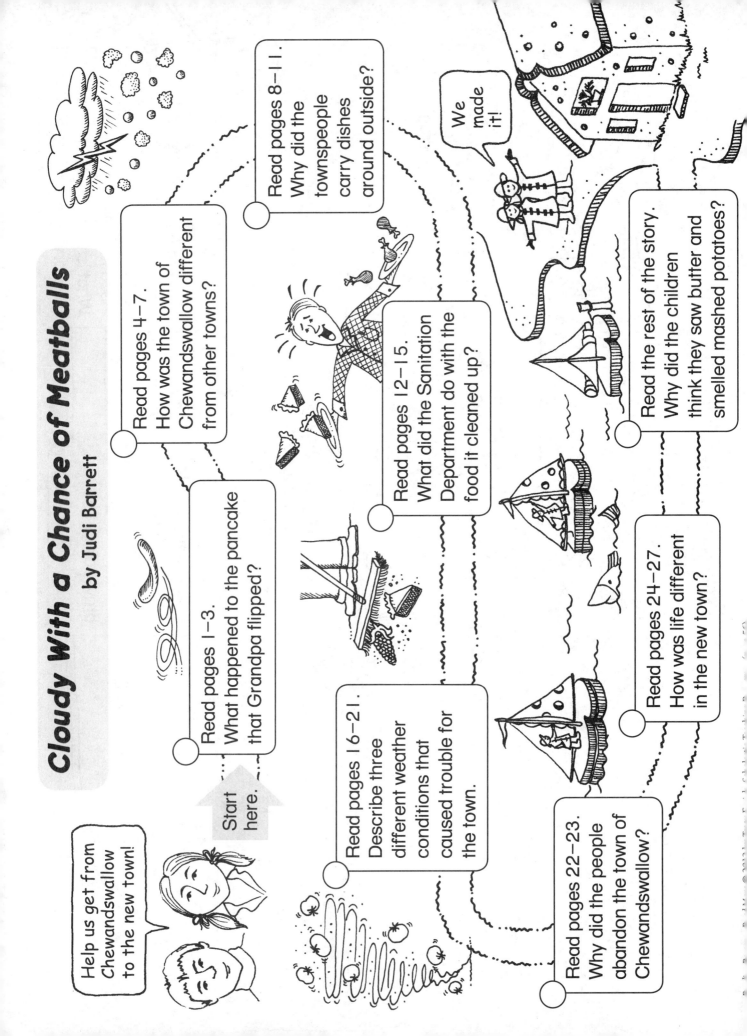

Cloudy With a Chance of Meatballs
by Judi Barrett

Help us get from Chewandswallow to the new town!

Start here.

Read pages 1–3.
What happened to the pancake that Grandpa flipped?

Read pages 4–7.
How was the town of Chewandswallow different from other towns?

Read pages 8–11.
Why did the townspeople carry dishes around outside?

Read pages 12–15.
What did the Sanitation Department do with the food it cleaned up?

Read pages 16–21.
Describe three different weather conditions that caused trouble for the town.

Read pages 22–23.
Why did the people abandon the town of Chewandswallow?

Read pages 24–27.
How was life different in the new town?

Read the rest of the story.
Why did the children think they saw butter and smelled mashed potatoes?

We made it!

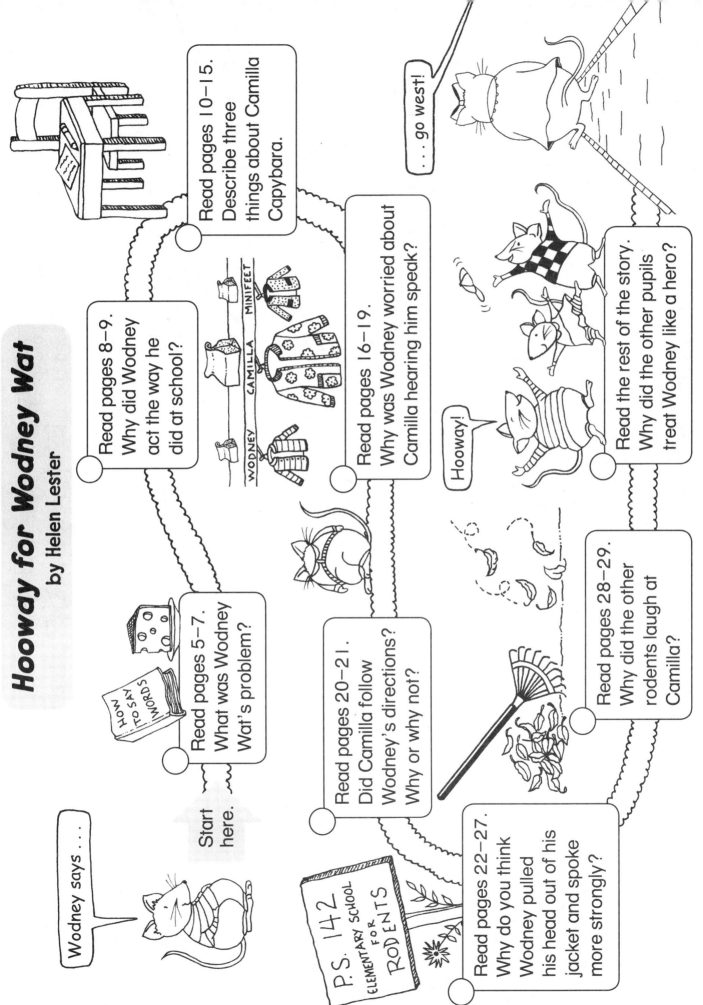

Hooway for Wodney Wat
by Helen Lester

Wodney says . . .

Start here.

Read pages 5–7. What was Wodney Wat's problem?

Read pages 8–9. Why did Wodney act the way he did at school?

Read pages 10–15. Describe three things about Camilla Capybara.

. . . go west!

Read pages 16–19. Why was Wodney worried about Camilla hearing him speak?

Read pages 20–21. Did Camilla follow Wodney's directions? Why or why not?

Read pages 22–27. Why do you think Wodney pulled his head out of his jacket and spoke more strongly?

Read pages 28–29. Why did the other rodents laugh at Camilla?

Read the rest of the story. Why did the other pupils treat Wodney like a hero?

Hooway!

P.S. 142 ELEMENTARY SCHOOL FOR RODENTS

WODNEY   CAMILLA   MINIFEET

HOW TO SAY WORDS

A Picture Book of Abraham Lincoln
by David Adler

Help me find my hat.

Start here.

Read pages 1–4. Name two states that Abraham Lincoln lived in as a boy.

Read pages 5–6. What did Abe like to do when he was a boy?

Read pages 7–10. Why do you think Abraham would never forget what he saw in New Orleans?

Read pages 11–14. Tell about three things that happened in Abraham's life on these pages.

Read pages 15–18. Why do you think the southern states formed their own government? Was this a good idea? Why or why not?

Read pages 19–24. What did the Emancipation Proclamation do? Why do you think Lincoln wrote it?

Read the rest of the story. What happened to Lincoln at the theater? Why did so many people go out to say good-bye to the President?

My hat!

Emancipation Proclamation

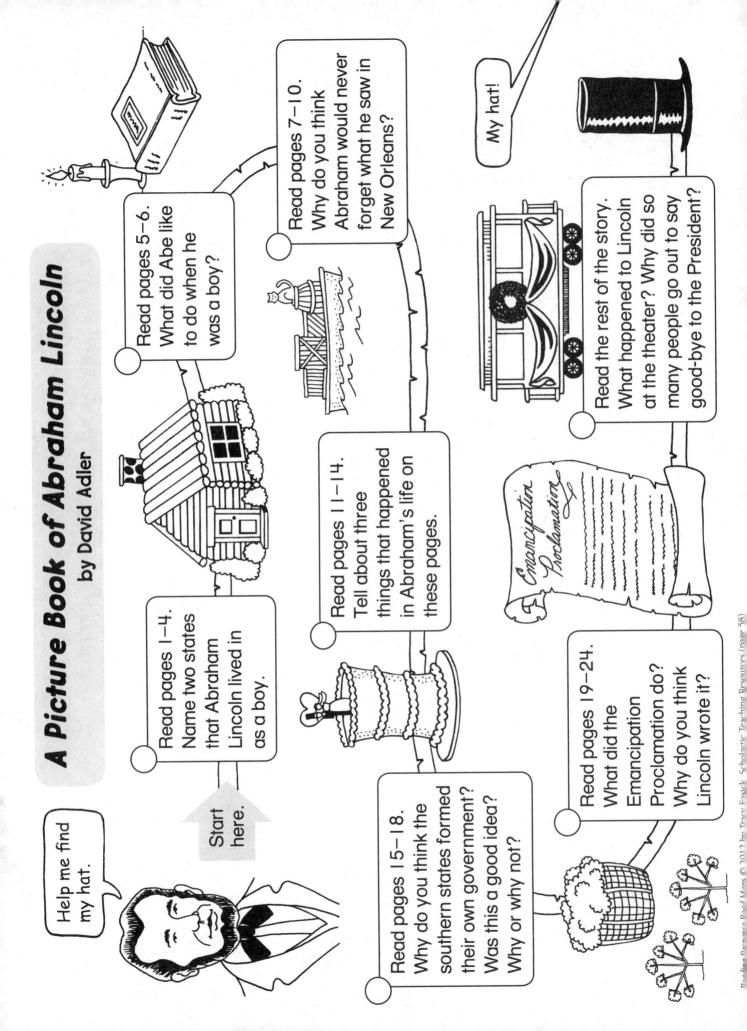

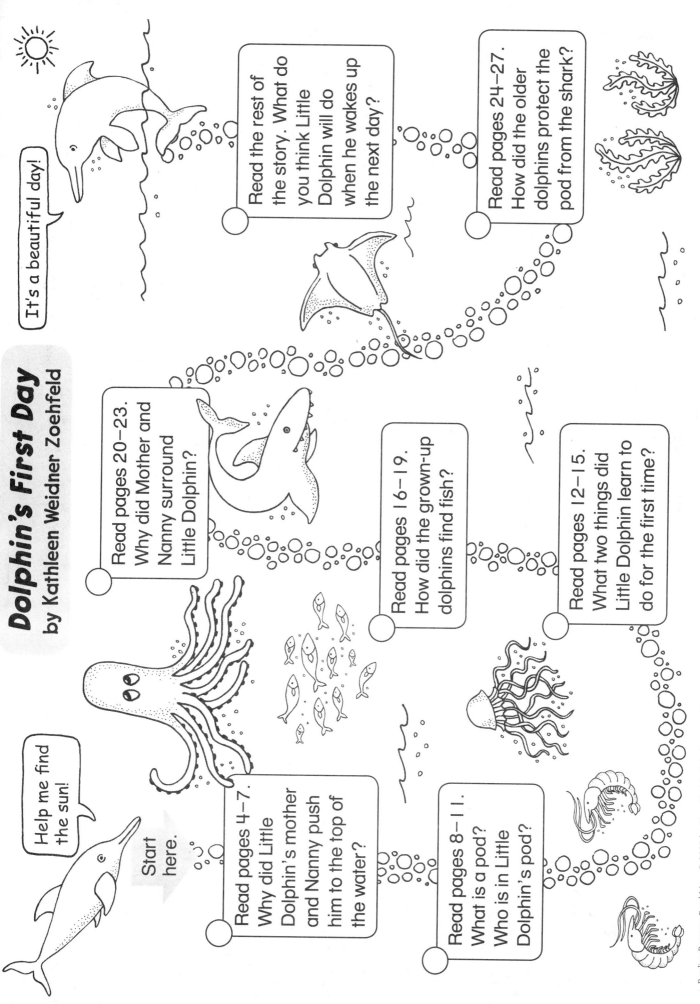

Dolphin's First Day
by Kathleen Weidner Zoehfeld

It's a beautiful day!

Help me find the sun!

Start here.

Read pages 4–7. Why did Little Dolphin's mother and Nanny push him to the top of the water?

Read pages 8–11. What is a pod? Who is in Little Dolphin's pod?

Read pages 12–15. What two things did Little Dolphin learn to do for the first time?

Read pages 16–19. How did the grown-up dolphins find fish?

Read pages 20–23. Why did Mother and Nanny surround Little Dolphin?

Read the rest of the story. What do you think Little Dolphin will do when he wakes up the next day?

Read pages 24–27. How did the older dolphins protect the pod from the shark?

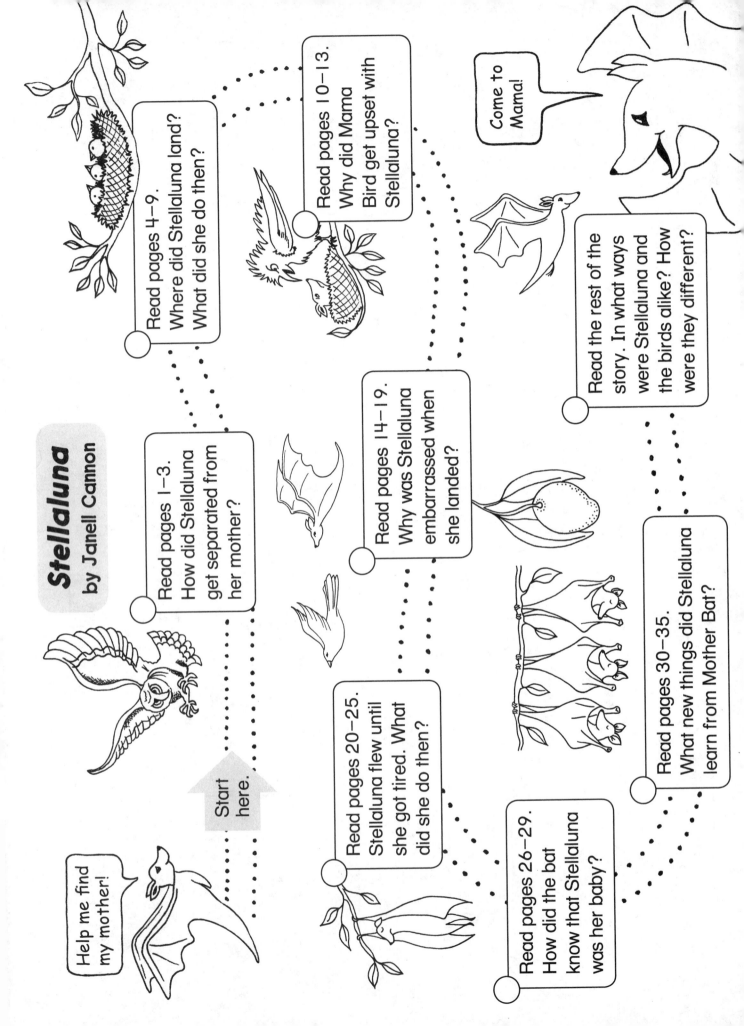

Stellaluna
by Janell Cannon

Help me find my mother!

Start here.

Read pages 1–3. How did Stellaluna get separated from her mother?

Read pages 4–9. Where did Stellaluna land? What did she do then?

Read pages 10–13. Why did Mama Bird get upset with Stellaluna?

Come to Mama!

Read the rest of the story. In what ways were Stellaluna and the birds alike? How were they different?

Read pages 14–19. Why was Stellaluna embarrassed when she landed?

Read pages 20–25. Stellaluna flew until she got tired. What did she do then?

Read pages 26–29. How did the bat know that Stellaluna was her baby?

Read pages 30–35. What new things did Stellaluna learn from Mother Bat?

The Gym Teacher From the Black Lagoon
by Mike Thaler

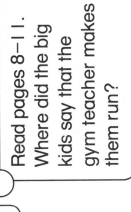

Hi! I'm your new gym teacher!

Read pages 8–11. Where did the big kids say that the gym teacher makes them run?

Read pages 4–7. Do you think the boy was afraid of the new gym teacher?

Read pages 1–3. What did the kids say about the new gym teacher?

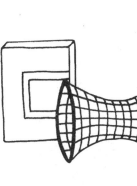

Read pages 12–15. Why would kids still be up in the ceiling of the gym?

Read the rest of the story. Why was the boy surprised when he met the gym teacher?

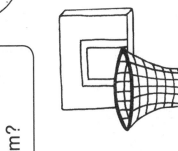

Read pages 16–21. What was the most outrageous thing that the gym teacher made the kids do? Explain why you think so.

Read pages 22–27. Do you think the big kids were telling the truth about the gym teacher? Why or why not?

Help me find the new gym teacher.

Start here.

The Milk Makers
by Gail Gibbons

Help the calf find its mommy.

Read pages 1–3. Dairy cows make milk. Name three other animals that make milk.

Start here.

Read pages 4–7. Why does a cow need to eat good foods?

Read pages 8–11. Why does a cow need to be milked twice a day?

Here I am, baby. Moo!

Read pages 12–15. Why do most farmers use milking machines?

Read pages 16–19. Why do you think the milk at the dairy is put in refrigerated tanks?

Read pages 20–23. Why are dates printed on milk jugs and cartons?

Read the rest of the story. Why is it important for the dairy workers to clean and sterilize the equipment?

MILK

MILK

MILK

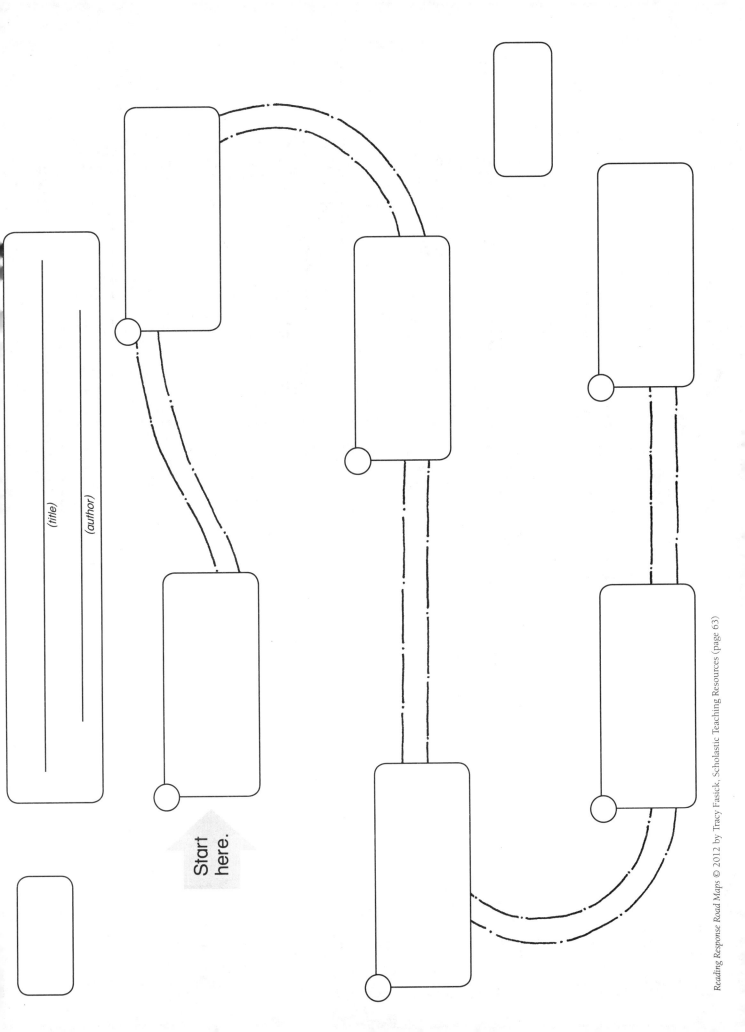

(title)

(author)

Start here.

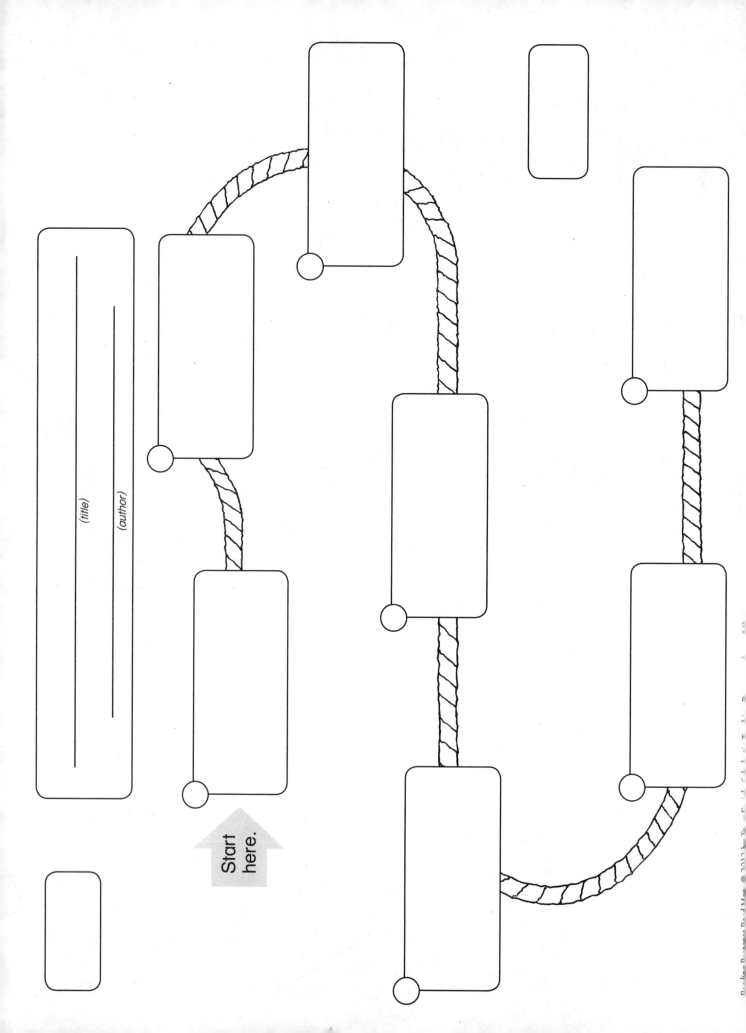

(title)

(author)

Start here.